ECO-NOMICS AND EAGLES

ECO-NOMICS AND EAGLES

A People's Guide to Economic Development <u>and</u> the Environment.

Kate Troll

Copyright © 2002 by Kate Troll.

Library of Congress Number: 2003090286

ISBN: Hardcover 1-4010-9285-3
Softcover 1-4010-9284-5

All rights reserved. No part of this book may be reproduced or transmitted in any form or by any means, electronic or mechanical, including photocopying, recording, or by any information storage and retrieval system, without permission in writing from the copyright owner.

This book was printed in the United States of America.

To order additional copies of this book, contact:
Xlibris Corporation
1-888-7-XLIBRIS
www.Xlibris.com
Orders@Xlibris.com
17120

CONTENTS

Chapter 1 9
   What Good Is An Eagle?
Chapter 2 22
   The Call to Arms and Peace
Chapter 3 38
   The Schooling Effect of Fish Politics
Chapter 4 50
   Sharing the Sound Responsibly
Chapter 5 61
   The Attraction of Lawsuit Avoidance
Chapter 6 74
   Beyond the Forest Wars:
   Respect and Ecosystem Management
Chapter 7 94
   Ecology Is Economy Is Ecology
Chapter 8 110
   Navigating the Extremes
Chapter 9 121
   Leadership That Says 'Yes' to Eco-nomics
Chapter 10 132
   Think Local—Act Global
Chapter 11 143
   Holding On to Leopold
Epilogue 151
   The Mountain Made Me Do It
Endnotes 159
Appendix A 168

Dedicated to Denali, the mountain within,
and to Erin and Rion, two awesome representatives
of the millennium generation.

CHAPTER 1

What Good Is An Eagle?

Many people know Haines, Alaska as the place where you get off the Alaska State Ferry and begin the Alaska Highway trek to Anchorage. But to me, Haines represents my first trial by fire and where I fell in love with Alaska. Haines holds some of the best of Alaska—rugged, majestic peaks, glaciers, wild rivers, dense forests, and cozy coastline. Anyone who has ever seen the movie *White Fang* will know what I'm talking about.

The resource conflict in Haines is the type of conflict still echoing through many small towns across rural America. In 1979, Haines was a timber town with a closed sawmill. Log shortages and Environmental Protection Agency permit problems were to blame. While a few town officials talked up the mission of economic diversification through fish processing and tourism, most "movers and shakers" acted like "screamers and railers." Screaming MORE WOOD! And railing against the EPA. It didn't take long before environmental bashing dominated community sentiment.

The conflict boiled down to one issue: either you supported the designation of all state lands for logging or you supported setting aside some state lands for the Haines Bald Eagle Preserve. Every autumn thousands of bald eagles converge along the river to feed on a late run of salmon—the world's largest concentration of eagles. Since those officials touting economic diversification had no concrete plan, environmental bashing held sway and any mention of the eagle preserve relegated one to the lowly status of "tree huggers." Does this conflict and name-calling sound familiar?

Perhaps in your region it's cranes and wetlands on one side and retirement community expansion on the other hand.

Even knowing these community dynamics, I found myself completely caught off-guard in my first public meeting as the city's hired planning consultant. I thought I was attending a preliminary meeting with the City Council to go over the scope of work and ground rules for drafting a Coastal Management Plan. Instead I found myself in a no holds barred public hearing about how coastal management related to the eagles and trees debate. In the midst of my preliminary explanation of the planning process, a scruffy, bearded logger wearing a wool red-checkered jacket rose up and interrupted with a question, "What good is an eagle if you can't eat it?"

I responded in my best professional voice, "I'd like to hold that question for a few minutes until I lay out the scope of work as the city requested." Dead silence. Soon the entire jam-packed room seemed to echo: "Enough of this planning BS. He asked a good question, "What good is an eagle if you can't eat it?" The mayor shrugged saying, "I think it's best if you just answer the question now."

Now, my unspoken gut response was, "What type of absurd question is this? Eagles are magnificent birds of prey, a sight to behold, our nation's symbol of freedom and patriotism, a part of this area's rich native heritage. You want to eat an eagle? Are you nuts?"

Yet, this logger was serious. He needed to keep his job, and from his perspective those eagles were taking food off his table. He had to earn a living. This was a question that my Yale Master's Degree hadn't prepared me for in the least. I took a moment to reflect. My answer would establish my professional credibility with this town. How could I answer honestly without alienating everybody?

Finally I answered, "Well, for one thing, eagles eat all the rotting salmon and the river would smell a whole lot worse without them." The logger responded, "So do bears, but I can eat them." The room shook with hoots and laughter. The bearded logger was enjoying a round of backslapping and high fives. I laughed with them at my expense. At least now I had time to think.

When the room quieted down, I focused on what I had overheard in the coffee shop earlier that day. "If you really do want to diversify your local economy," I told them, "you have to use of all your assets. You have the world's largest concentration of bald eagles. This is an economic asset. This is what sets you apart from other Southeast communities that compete for cruise ship traffic. Ketchikan has the native element with their totem pole collection. Sitka has the Russian historic twist; Juneau has the capitol and a road-accessible glacier. Skagway has the Chilkoot Trail and the gold rush. Haines has some of all this. Haines can make claims as to whose native history is more interesting or which glacier is more alluring, or Haines can capitalize on what no other coastal town has—a world-class natural history phenomenon that the average American can relate to. You may not be able to eat them, but if you work it right, the eagles just may be your most immediate ticket for new jobs that put food on the table." When I finished with a few examples about a visitor center and Audubon tours, a low buzz of conversation and head nodding went through the meeting room. Finally they let me proceed with the meeting agenda.

When I had time to reflect on the dynamics of this meeting, I realized that if I had justified the land allocation for the eagles out of the eagle's intrinsic natural value I would have bombed. But by portraying the eagles as an economic asset, the discussion shifted from eagles versus timber to eagles and timber. Not only had I passed my first professional trial by fire, I had generated one of those paradigm shifts that all the management consultants speak about at conferences. I shifted from balancing to synergy.

And it gave me a philosophy: Instead of viewing possible solutions to resource conflicts as just a search for fair and reasonable balance, I should search for the best ways to tap the synergy between environmental and economic concerns. Instead of looking for fair trade-offs between environment and economic values, I should be looking for ways to fuse agendas; to translate environmental concerns into economic matters and vice-versa. I continued to press this line of thinking as I circulated through town listening and conjecturing about eagle tourism (now called eco-tourism). Ultimately, the Haines Coastal Management Plan included tourism recommendations focused on the seasonal gathering of eagles in the Chilkat Valley. This plan was the first coastal management plan to be approved in Alaska.

In the twenty years since Haines, I have vastly expanded my resource/political horizons. There have been many such "linkage moments." These realizations have crystallized into a personal working philosophy to seek the special synergy between economic development and environmental protection. This book aims to share all the synergy I've found, explain how to find more, and lastly tell a few good stories along the way.

Connect community planning and economic theory with Ecology 101, and it becomes easier to see that healthy environments and stable economies have a yin-yang relationship. Stable, healthy ecosystems sustain economic communities. Stable economies foster better environmental practices than unstable, boom-and-bust economies. Stability of one system promotes stability in the other system. The renewability of our natural resources and the long-term viability of our air, water and land are more readily advanced by a caring society that has long-term economic growth and stability. And vice-versa, sustained and controlled growth comes only with thoughtful management of renewable resources and healthy ecosystems. The whole notion of sustainable development is founded on this yin-yang relationship.

Nurturing this relationship is what Alaska represents to me. Alaska is the place to do development right. Here in Alaska, the water is clean, the forest immense, the fisheries plentiful, the mountains rich, and the wildlife abundant. With the unlimited beauty and grandeur of Alaska percolating through my soul each weekend outing, I began to combine my love for the great outdoors with a professional drive to do right in and by Alaska; to take the lesson learned in Haines and start anew in the bounty of Alaska.

While in many regards, Alaska has it all and it's tempting to just hunker down and close off the rest of the world, I know all too well that economically and ecologically Alaska is connected to the rest of the world. For example, El Nino and the Asian economic flu both challenge the viability of our coastal fisheries. When the Berlin Wall came down, Alaskans were among the first to reestablish cultural and economic ties with Russia. British Petroleum owns our oil. Germans and Australians visit Alaska in droves. Even in Alaska, the economic woes of a country across the ocean can affect our daily life in much the same way that we feel the ecological shock waves from far away catastrophic events.

We live in global villages interconnected through economic and ecological systems. To capture this relationship as well as the paradigm shift in my thinking, I sketched out this symbol:

This is the yin of the earth and the yang represented by the symbol for the Euro, the new currency of Europe. This is also the symbol for a working vision that I call "eco-nomics." Eco-nomics means tapping into the synergy between sound economies and healthy ecosystems. Eco-nomics recognizes that it's impossible to have a sound economy without a sound environment. Similarly, environmental initiative can benefit from a sound economy. The trick is getting the public and those in decision-making capacities to recognize and act to promote this linkage. This means fusing the political agendas of disparate and often acrimonious interest groups. Not easy. Therefore, eco-nomics is also about techniques and insights into how best to achieve this goal of fusion. The "how" is explained through the use of nine principles. Following these principles puts you on the path of changing the jobs *versus* environment scenario into a jobs *and* the environment scenario. They help transform and lessen conflict. These eco-nomic principles come from understanding both systems, ecology and economics.

Alaska serves as an apt setting to bring forward these practical principles of eco-nomics into perspective. Nowhere else did Ralph Nader and the Green Party get ten percent of the 2000 vote. (Bush received fifty-nine percent.) Nowhere else are conflicts between developers and environmentalists more easily triggered than in Alaska. Even for Bush and Gore, Alaska served as an environmental litmus test. Unlike some campaign issues, the candidates clearly differed on the question of opening the Arctic National Wildlife Refuge to oil development. Alaska is good at bringing out the differences on a wide range of concerns.

"After all," explains Governor Jay Hammond, "the two types of people most inclined to come to the Great Land assure it. Along with the would-be rustics comes another type of pioneer no less determined to find a different kind of good life."[1] But just as land-use conflict is not confined to Alaska, the application and relevancy of these principles moves well beyond Alaska and on into addressing the environmental gap reflected in Election 2000.

But before I get too far ahead again, I want to return to the word "eco-nomics." I first coined this term out of a very practical need to avoid a "greenie" label that could essentially disarm my problem-solving proposals. A few years after my experience in Haines, I moved to Ketchikan, the first city one reaches in Alaska when traveling by ferry. Ketchikan, population 13,000, is at the southern end of the Tongass National Forest, the largest remaining temperate rain forest in North America. Timber, commercial fishing, tourism and government form the town's economic cornerstones, but Ketchikan's most noted feature is rain. For every one thousand people, there is a foot of rain every year. Ketchikan is the closest you can come to actually living underwater.

In 1981, I started working for the Ketchikan Planning and Zoning Department. After four months of meeting and working with the town's leadership, it was clear that I didn't quite fit in with the main interest groups. I sympathized with both sides of the development/protection issues. As a community planner this was okay because my job was to listen. Then I ran for local office and my job expanded to listening and leading. It didn't take long as a Borough Assembly Member (similar to County Commissioner) before I found myself continually fighting the Chamber of Commerce's disdainful "greenie" label. Even when my votes clearly showed I supported economic development, the Chamber types still dismissed my contribution as "nothing but green talk." At the same time my friends in the environmental community were disappointed that I didn't clearly support their efforts and their positions. Yet, when I talked one-on-one with community residents, I knew that I was tuned into their basic desires for job security and wanting to raise a family in a clean and healthy environment. It wasn't an either/or choice for them. They wanted both. I also realized that in Alaska the desire for a healthy environment means more than wanting safe drinking water. It means protecting the values that we all sought in coming to Alaska . . . the wildness, the fishing and hunting, the grand beauty. Jobs and the environment were in the hearts of most residents, but the organized, vocal groups insisted on putting residents into an either/or situation. Either you were with the pulp mill one hundred percent or you were against it. Either you wanted to stop all logging or you were a rape and pillage advocate. There was simply no voice for the middle ground.

I was lost in the silent majority. To give myself some reference in the vacuum of the middle, I coined the term "enviro-nomics" (later changed to eco-nomics in the evolutionary process of ideas). The term shielded me from being easily labeled as being on one side or the other. They had to ask themselves, "Hmm, what does she mean when she says she advocates an eco-nomic solution?"

When I presented my own label, I found audiences less likely to judge my words based on an inappropriate label. However, it wasn't until I completed my term on the Borough Assembly and took a job with the commercial salmon industry that I found organizational support for eco-nomic positions on resource issues.

Commercial fishermen are sometimes viewed in the West as marine cowboys, hustling fish in the great open ocean pastures. But to many people's surprise, these same marine cowboys are often the first to speak out about habitat protection and conservation. In Alaska, where the seafood industry is the state's largest private sector employer, fishermen have a strong voice and often acted as the broker between development interests and environmentalists. In Alaska, the salmon fishermen know that "habitat is where it's at."

Through the ecologically tuned-in fishermen, I learned that eco-nomics was real and could be actively practiced. Nonetheless, going public at the time with the term enviro-nomics was another matter, as it tended to generate raised eyebrows and snickers. Maybe it was just small-town politics in Alaska. It just sounded too ivory tower. Besides most people did not know that I had a Master's Degree from Yale School of Forestry and Environmental Studies. In Alaska, unlike most places where you establish yourself on educational and professional credentials, one establishes oneself by length of residency, property ownership and number of children. Announcing that I had a degree from Yale would be the kiss of death in many a local hearing. So naturally the ivory tower connotation of the word eco-nomics made me hesitant to use the term, much less espouse an eco-nomic vision.

Then the rubber hit the road when I was selected to testify before the U.S. Senate Energy and Natural Resources Committee on the Tongass Timber Reform Act. The act would determine the management direction for the Tongass Forest and affect all of the communities in Southeast Alaska. I represented the United Fishermen of Alaska, an umbrella organization made up of twenty-three regional fishing associations. The room was packed.

C-Span cameras, bright lights and the formally seated Senate committee created an intimidating atmosphere. I felt myself beginning to clutch. Then I realized that I would testify after my hometown nemesis who always said the right thing to get me up on step back home in Ketchikan. In fact, I was in the enviable position of testifying fourth, or as I preferred to see it, I was batting clean up. Control and confidence began to seep back into me. My mind began to spin: "Hey, I could pick up all the contentious pieces and close with my enviro-nomic philosophy. Dare I? In front of the national press, in front of all these VIP strangers? After all, I was going to establish my Yale credentials in my opening remarks . . . no need to worry about sounding too ivory tower here." A little voice inside stirred, "It's time to lay it on the line."

So I did. I took a deep breath and launched into the completion of my testimony:

> "In closing, I am going to get a bit philosophical. The challenge of the 1990s is to find the balance between economics and environment, what I call the 'enviro-nomic' solution. There are ways to protect the environment without causing massive layoffs, such as buffers along salmon streams. There are long-term economic payoffs for key watershed protection, such as dollars back in tourism and fish. The economy and the environment are linked, not diametrically opposed. It is time to promote the linkages in any and all legislation that comes before this committee. You no longer have the luxury of passing separate jobs and wilderness legislation. The needs of the economy and environmental protection must be weighed simultaneously. As you know, the Tongass Timber Reform Act is only one example of the eco-nomic challenge of the 1990s.
>
> "Finding the balance between economics and environment can be a difficult task, as it demands an empathy for the working man and woman, and a vision for our environmental future. But you have two useful guides in

finding the solution for the Tongass—the position of the United Fishermen of Alaska and the original Southeast Conference (an umbrella organization for the municipal governments in Southeast Alaska) position. Like the fishermen in Alaska, most Americans want to be gainfully employed while raising their families in a clean and prosperous environment. Like the fishermen in Alaska, polls show that most Americans are now willing to accept paying the economic costs of protecting the environment. Like the fishermen in Alaska many now sense the inescapable linkage between a stable economy and a healthy environment. It is time to cast a new image for Alaska land legislation. Cast away the image of Alaska being a battleground for development versus wilderness and replace it with the image of Alaska being the breaking ground for the 'enviro-nomic' balance."

At the close of my testimony, Senator Bennett Johnson, the chair from Louisiana, gave me my shot at national recognition. He leaned over my way and said, "I have one question and one comment for this witness. Did you say you have a master's from the Yale School of Forestry? And I like that enviro-nomics stuff. Staff make note of that for me." YESSS! I answered while pumping my fist in celebration below the witness table.

Two weeks later the committee passed out a new draft of the Tongass Timber Reform Act; a draft modeled after United Fishermen of Alaska's recommendation. That same month, I found myself in Haines on fish business. I found brochures proclaiming the unique wonders of the Haines Bald Eagle Preserve. New tour businesses and an eagle visitor center had been built. Cruise ships were stopping. The mill operated intermittently. Ah yes, things seemed right in my world of Southeast Alaska. In fact, things seemed right for eco-nomics to move forward into a more complete working vision for me as a resource professional . . . a vision kindled by the question of "What Good Is an Eagle?" and justified in the brief comment and action of an influential U.S. Senator.

Through the years, I have refined and expanded my working vision through experience, study, mentors and mountains. And through this refinement and expansion process, enviro-nomics naturally morphed into a more holistic... "eco-nomics." The association was also clearer for conveying the nine principles of linkage.

This book represents an honest effort to bring my vision of eco-nomics to other similarly engaged citizens and resource professionals. I hope that the principles of eco-nomics will work for many responsible residents of this Earth. Responsibility in this context means believing and trusting in human power to ethically restore nature.

Can you see yourself in the morning mirror of honesty as a fellow human being capable of the power to do right by nature? Can you admit that we have wised up from the days of sanctioned pollution that compelled Rachel Carson to write *Silent Spring*? Rachel Carson warned us in a 1963 television interview with CBS that: "Man is a part of nature, and his war against nature is inevitably a war against himself." We no longer wage a war to conquer and indiscriminately pollute nature because in those famous words of Pogo, we have seen the enemy and it is us. Now is the time to take the words of Rachel Carson to the next level, to renewing ourselves through restoring nature and believing in our ability to do so. This is the underlying premise for accepting a place for eco-nomics.

If you can agree with these words of environmental reporter Walter Truett Anderson, then the principles of eco-nomics may apply in your business, community or professional endeavors:

> "The back-to-nature mystique is based on opposition to human power in nature, and its followers are always reluctant to acknowledge having any themselves. We have to admit to having power, face the impossibility of leaving nature alone, and cultivate our environmental ethics and policies accordingly."[2]

Indeed, it has even been argued by some economists that the environmental protection existing today is a product of and not a reaction to industrial development... that through industrialization we have the luxury to care and the power to change. Industrialization creates the arena for society to demand environmental protection measures from companies. Industrialization also brings technology, and as technological advancements cross-fertilize from one field to another as in laser optics to bioengineering, so grow the opportunities for more environmental protection.

"The future will likely belong to what I call proactive environmentalists," notes reporter Anderson, "people who are able to use information and technology, and who don't mind living in this world as it is, and who are unafraid to engage in the hands-on management of ecosystems."[3]

There is no just "going back to nature" just like it's foolish to wage a war against nature and ourselves. There should be no ethical quandary about the use of proven, safe environmental technology. We live in a world molded by the power of humans and now it's time to use this power to better mold and restore nature. Just as we recognize that wilderness has it own place in a stewardship-minded, civilized society, so too should we recognize that man, and all that come with him, has his unique place among Earth's natural residents. Environmental technology and ecosystem management should be embraced, not feared or loathed.

Certainly government regulation and oversight is and will continue to be a primary means of getting companies and jurisdictions to employ environmental management and engineering. Government plays a critical role in prompting and defining the environmental sideboards that in turn allows for the marketplace to play a bigger role. And although there is still historical distrust of "big business," most Americans think local businesses are doing their share to reduce environmental problems. The annual environment survey done by Wirthlin Worldwide shows that fifty-five percent think that local business is either doing the right amount or more than its share to reduce environmental problems.⁴ This compares to a fifty percent favorable rating for state and local government doing their part.⁵ This suggests to me that public perception can match what is functionally best for government and business—a partnership for the environment. I say "can match" because the same survey shows large corporations lag significantly in favorable public opinion and are perceived as putting profits well ahead of other considerations. Nonetheless, the marketplace is embracing environmental technology and management as noted by economist and author Michael Silverstein:

> "The best and brightest in the American marketplace soon enough realized that what others were lamenting as a 'forced,' regulation-induced, diet like change advanced a larger market agenda and their own best interest. They came to identify environmental economics as just plain old good economics; environmental engineering as superior engineering; and environmental management as quality management."⁶

There are now many economic incentives in play for corporations to act more responsibly toward the environment. And as chapter seven reveals, responsible corporations do indeed exist . . . they are not all Enron's and WorldCom's.

I recognize that to seek linkage instead of polarity, and to recognize ecosystems and economic health as ebbing and flowing in tandem, requires perspectives and attitudes to shift. To make this shift doable for as many walks of life as possible, I have rooted these eco-nomic principles in the belief that man's heart is good; that man's intellect spurs technological and scientific wisdom for sustainable living and restoration; that the marketplace along with government can succeed in implementing this wisdom.

CHAPTER 2

The Call to Arms and Peace

The Call to Arms

"This is a war zone. Our goal is to destroy, to eradicate the environmental movement," claims Ron Arnold, founder of the Wise Use Movement. "What you have to realize is the reason that we have no jobs is because of the environmental laws. It's become a green depression caused by environmental over regulation."[7]

On the western front, J. Robert Cox, President of the Sierra Club responds: "Americans did not sign a contract for America in November [1994] to dismantle three decades of environmental protection. Working together we can reverse the tide of this war on the environment."[8]

So which is it? Wise Use or Sierra Club? Or in more rural communities it might be more appropriate to ask: Which is it? Chamber of Commerce or Friends of . . . (you fill in the blank).

As public lands are increasingly managed to enhance recreation and protect wildlife, rural communities, particularly in the West, face transformation issues that resonate in conflict. Take, for example, this exchange between a realtor named Hank, who serves as the sergeant-at-arms at the local Elks club, and Judith. Judith is a librarian by day and a Conservation Director by night. Whose friend are you? Hank or Judith's?

Hank: "Industrial waterfront is getting hard to find. This zoning proposal makes good sense but I hear we can expect a battle. We can't let those imported 'tree huggers' beat us in our own backyard.

It's time to draw the line at the city limits. This is our town and I want to see economic opportunity for our kids."

Judith: "I can't believe these yo-yos want to zone all the remaining natural waterfront industrial. Don't they care about the future of this town and how it's going to look. Green space goes a long way in returning value to Riverside. The last thing we need is more polluting industry. Hey, I have an idea. Let's put in our own proposal to counter theirs. Let's ask for a public recreation designation instead. We can beat the Chamber of Horrors at their own zoning game."

The next morning on the call-in radio show, the debate heats up:

Hank on the AM station's Problem Corner: "I hear ya Ma'am. If we let these know-it-all greenies have their way, they'll turn the whole darn town into a park. I grew up in this country—had my first job on the Rolling River Barge. And let me tell you, there's plenty of wild country left along our river. Besides you can't feed a family on scenery. But what do they know? They're all just a bunch of outsiders anyway."

Judith on the FM station's Morning Coffee Call In: "The recreational proposal submitted by the Friends of the River would only bring Riverside up to .2 acres of parkss and recreation land per capita; still below the national average for a town the size of Riverside. We're the reasonable ones here. We just want what's healthy and natural. Who knows? If the chamber had their way they'd probably fill all the remaining waterfront. And what for? Industries that pollute. If that's what they want, let then move to Houston."

Do you know a Hank or Judith in your town or neighborhood? Does this exchange ring at all familiar to you? It does to me. For the past dozen or so years I have witnessed the non-stop launching of rhetoric rockets between the camps of pro-developers and environmentalists. The rockets are launched in all forms and in all forums. Sometimes they hit their target dead center and generate counterattacks. Sometimes they fizzle out or even backfire.

Sometimes the rhetoric gets downright petty. Sometimes I think we never quite grow up. But I know better. It's not immaturity. Rather, it is a rock-hard passion for the land and a fierce sense of frontier independence, which drives the third-generation rancher and local environmentalist into a grudge match of escalating proportions. It's a call to arms that ripples through small towns across America and into the arena of national politics. Take a look at these headlines:

W's Green War

Any color but green
A new political alliance is battling the environmental movement

On the Western Front
Dispatches from the war with the Wise Use Movement

The War Among the Greens
Grassroots environmentalists charge 'sellout'

BABBITT'S RETREAT

New environmental war targets Northwest salmon

Congressional Chain-Saw Massacre
If Speaker Newt Gingrich gets his way, the laws protecting air, water and wildlife may be endangered.

Greenpeace Takes Over the World

Is it any wonder that it seems like America is on the brink of a new cold war? Hardly a month goes by when I don't encounter a byline on the environment with a military metaphor.

Which came first, the local debate or the national clash of economic development versus environmental protection? Hmm . . . can you imagine a debate between presidential candidates Al Gore and George W. Bush on just the subject of the environment? I think it would be as lively as a local showdown in a small, mountain town but instead of the town hall setting, the setting would probably be a national talk show, like *Larry King Live*. While Al Gore didn't want to do the talk show rounds with George W. Bush, we can easily cut and slice from their stump speeches, books and interviews to get a sense of how such a debate would play out. What transpires below is just that—a weaving together of actual quotes from George W. Bush and Al Gore placed in the fictional setting of *Larry King Live*.

To better illuminate the national boundaries of the jobs versus environment debate, the Sierra Club and the Wise Use Movement also joined the show. Here's the clip of the national clash mirroring the Hank and Judith debate on economic development versus the environment:

Larry King: "Vice President Gore, as the author of *Earth in the Balance* you've sort of set yourself up as an expert and an environmental target."

Gore: "My adversaries, some of whom I suspect haven't read it, love to hate this book and attack it as too environmental. I welcome that. I believe the environment should be a central issue in the year 2000 because, like it or not, the environment will be a fateful issue in the next decade and the new century."[9]

King: "And one of these fateful issues I presume is global warming. Governor Bush what about global warming?"

Bush: "It's an issue we need to take very seriously. I don't think we know the solution to global warming yet and I don't think we've got all the facts before we make decisions."[10]

Gore, with a subdued chuckle interrupts: "I disagree that we don't know the cause of global warming. I think that we do. It's pollution, carbon dioxide and other chemicals that are even more potent. Look, the world's temperature is going up, weather patterns are changing, storms are getting more violent and unpredictable. And what are we going to tell our children?"[11]

Bush: "Yeah, I agree in part. Some of the scientists, I believe haven't they been changing their opinion a little bit on global warming? There's a lot of differing opinions and before we react I think it's best to have the full accounting, full understanding of what's taking place."[12]

King: "Let's move on to issues closer to home. Governor Bush you unveiled a proposal to prescribe flexible standards and technology as the best antidote for pollution and blight.

Bush: "Yes, I pledge, if elected to eliminate red tape and give states the money and regulatory flexibility to clean up polluted sites. Texas didn't wait for Al Gore to wave his magic wand to clean up our environment. We cleaned it up ourselves, and our state's the better for it."[13]

Gore: "My opponent is the governor of the smoggiest state with the smoggiest city in the country. His idea of environmental protection is putting big polluters in charge of environmental laws."[14]

Bush: "Not true. The solution is not to eliminate the federal role in protecting the environment. The solution is reform that sets high standards."[15]

Larry interrupts: "And now for a word from our sponsors. But stay tuned. When we come back, we'll have the Sierra Club taking on the Wise Use Movement."

For a change, two commercials provide a win-win message about environmental responsibility. First, there is a powerful pitch by Du Pont Chemicals marketing its environmental remediation services worldwide. Next is a warm and fuzzy spot produced by 3M company explaining how they initiated a pollution-prevention program to cut waste and in the process saved $500 million in operating costs.[16]

King: "And now back to the greater call to arms. I want you to meet Ron Arnold and Chuck Cushman, the founders of the Wise Use

Movement. The Wise Use Movement acts as a national umbrella group for a wide range of organizations and extractive resource industries that feel government is stepping on their rights to use private and public lands. It has a broad base of major organizations including the Farm Bureau Federation, the National Rifle Association, the Cattleman's Association, American Mining Congress, Independent Petroleum Association of America and the American Land Rights Association. The Wise Use Movement was born in nineteen eighty-eight, when two hundred fifty groups met in Bellevue, Washington to find a common ground from which to fight environmentalism. Ron Arnold heads the Center for the Defense of Free Enterprise, one of the groups under the Wise Use umbrella, while Chuck Cushman leads another group, the National Inholders Association. Welcome gentlemen to the program.

"On the other side of this evening's debate, we have two Sierra Club representatives, Executive Director Carl Pope and Past President Michelle Perrault. Now, most people have heard about the Sierra Club; but for those in the audience unfamiliar with it, naturalist John Muir founded the Sierra Club in eighteen ninety-two. From its origin in California, the Sierra Club has expanded to become one of the most powerful environmental organizations in the country with members throughout the world. They address a broad range of environmental concerns from wilderness to community recycling. Also on the program tonight is Richard Stapleton, writer and producer of *Down to Earth* a daily environmental broadcast for CBS Radio News. Welcome ladies and gentlemen.

"Let's start with the hot topic debate that has been festering for years in Washington and Oregon. Ron your take on the endangered spotted owl?"

Arnold: "I'm sure everybody has heard of the spotted owl. Well, when it was listed even though there were eleven thousand of them in Washington State where I happen to live, loggers just simply lost their jobs in one day. People don't matter anymore to environmentalists. They're destroying the American economy, and I am not going to let them do that."[17]

Stapleton: "The fight is not over jobs. Those loggers in Portland are out of work despite the fact that cutting in Oregon's national forests has increased 16 percent in the past decade, Environmentalism is not their problem; exportation and automation are. The Wise Use Movement is clever, callous, politically astute, and very well funded. It is the dark side of conservation, environmentalism's evil enemy."[18]

Larry: "Mr. Cushman, your nickname is Mr. Rent-A-Riot. Would you care to respond?"

Cushman: "If we're the dark force, preservation is a new religion, a new paganism, that worships trees and sacrifices people. It's not only property or jobs but that special kind of relationship with people that we're trying to save. People are part of the environment! [And in regards to my nickname] I'm on a mission to keep rural America alive. I'm in the confrontation business. That's what I do. It's just like Patton standing out there. I'm the tank commander."[19]

Pope from the Sierra Club injects: "This is what makes the Sierra Club's traditional conservation agenda more vital than ever. We are going to the courts, to Congress, to the public, and to the media to explain the threats of [what we call] the Land Abuse Coalition."[20]

King: "Whoa, what about compromise, working things out? Michelle Perrault, we haven't heard from you yet. What does the Sierra Club think about compromising with these folks?"

Perrault: "A lot of people have this idea that consensus is wonderful. Sure we need to talk with developers who are opposed to us, but it's ludicrous to think we must weigh all views equally, because unwise development has destroyed so much already. The President needs to do less balancing and make hard decisions that may offend powerful people."[21]

King: "Mr. Cushman, what's the Wise Use Movement's take on compromising with the environmental community?"

Cushman: "Compromising with environmentalists leads to a gradual, systematic regulatory blanket of red tape which strangles everything you do and everything your family does in your future and for other generations."[22]

King: "Well, that certainly doesn't sound very promising. Maybe, now is a good time to go back to our presidential candidates for some thoughts on the role of government and regulation. We'll start with Governor Bush. Your thoughts on this topic sir?

Bush: "The federal government has a crucial role to play in conservation, particularly in managing our national forests, our park system, wilderness areas and national wildlife refuges. But problems arise when leaders reject partnership and rely solely on the power of Washington; on regulations, penalties and dictation from afar."[23]

Gore anxious to weigh in: "The big lie in this debate is that a good environment is bad economics. We've had the strongest economy in the world, while we've repeatedly strengthened environmental protection all across the board. In the long run, protecting our economy and preserving the environment go hand in hand and we cannot have one without the other."[24]

King: "Well on that 'hand in hand' note, let me extend my thanks to our presidential candidates for readjusting their schedules to join us tonight. It was good to have both of you here. That's all the time we have. This has been *Larry King Live*. Thanks for joining us.

What do you think of such a talk show? Maybe a show like this would air out some of the rhetoric behind the nasty headlines. So much of our political process feeds on conflict. In the world of twenty-four-hour news, seven days a week, it's not surprising that much of the media looks for opportunities to fan the flames of conflict.

For one example of our political propensity for conflict, look at the web sites of the two political parties. The Democratic Party's web site has assembled facts illuminating Bush's anti-environment record. One item reports that over 2,500 premature deaths in Texas were linked to air pollution in 1999.[25] On the Republican side, the GOP web site features "Gore's Unnatural Environmental Hysteria".[26] Talk show aside, the bottom line is, if you're into social conflict whether on a local or national level, the environment is and will likely remain a hot-button issue generating intense feelings, at least until we begin to change the language and the perception of conflict.

The People's Call to Peace

In 1992, I attended a conference billed as the "Needs of the Nineties: Prosperity and Protection." I thought I might meet and learn from like-minded people who saw the hand-in-hand approach of the economy and the environment. Wrong! With few exceptions, the conference speakers railed on about the evils of environmentalism.

As the rhetoric of intolerance escalated at the conference, I moved to the back row. I had enough of prosperity versus protection and began audibly groaning at the outbursts. Others in the back row began moaning in disgust. Soon there was a small chorus of attendees moaning, "C'mon let's be reasonable." Some conference attendees even started walking out. Wow, I was not alone after all! I was not the only one tuning out the rabble-rousing speaker. Spurred by this reaction, I thought it would be interesting to research the prevailing American attitudes about the environment and development. On my first foray to the library, I discovered that we back row moaners were in-sync with what most Americans thought about the economy and the environment.

First, I found the Environmental Forum Survey, conducted by the Roper Organization and commissioned for *Times Mirror Magazines*. This survey found that for three years in a row, 66 percent of Americans believed environmental protection and economic development went hand in hand, concluding: "Almost every American (89 percent in 1994) feels that we can find a balance that allows us to enjoy economic progress while making sure our rivers, lakes, mountains and wildlife are protected."[27]

The Environmental Forum also noted that while 72 percent of Americans consider themselves conservationists, they also believe that through sound management we can both protect and enjoy the use of natural resources. Furthermore, the survey revealed that Americans are seeking pragmatic solutions that balance environmental and economic concerns. "Extremists at either end of the environmental spectrum don't have much sway with the American public, which considers itself pro-conservation."[28]

A February 2000 survey conducted by Greenberg Quinlan Research at the request of the League of Conservation Voters concurs with these survey results: "Nearly three quarters (74 percent) of both moderates and liberal voters and 68 percent of conservative voters believe that America can have a clean environment and a strong economy without having to choose one over the other."[29] These results indicate that on face-value of the economy and the environment, Americans see them as one and the same.

Are you surprised by these poll findings? I was. Encouraged, I sought out more polling results. The more I dug, the more linkage support I found. In 1997, Wirthlin Worldwide, an international research and consulting company, concluded from their systematic annual surveys that: a) the 90s have been characterized by a more moderate view that it is possible to balance environmental protection and economic growth and b) seven out of ten Americans agree that it does not necessarily have to be a choice between the two."[30] In 1998 the Wirthlin Group reported 75 percent of Americans feel it was possible to find a balance between a strong economy and a clean environment.[31]

This trend of Americans seeing linkage between the economy and the environment also came through in the 2000 Presidential Vote. CNN exit's polls showed that six out of ten voters who said economy/jobs mattered most, voted for Al Gore, the environmental candidate.[32] The exit polls also showed a big split in the urban and rural vote, with large and small city residents siding with Gore and the small town, rural resident favoring Bush. I don't find this too surprising and it may suggest that this "linkage" trend weakens as one moves from the city to the country. Regardless, Election 2000 is seen by many as a milestone election for the environment.

"We think this was a historical election for the environment," claims Deb Callahan, League of Conservation Voters president. "The environment played a bigger role in more campaigns and at a higher level than it ever has before."[33] Polls by Business Week/Harris Poll confirm Callahan's post-election assessment. A Harris poll found that 63 percent of declared voters said the environment was a very important issue in determining whom they voted for in major political offices.[34] Wow, that's sixty-three percent of the voting populace who said the environment mattered to them when they stepped into the voting booth. Four years earlier, or in 1996, the environment was at best a side issue important in some regions and in some races.

Besides these illuminating election/survey results, the spoiler role played by the Green Party also makes Election 2000 a standout election for the environment. We would have a different President today had Ralph Nader not received over 96,000 votes in the crucial state of Florida. For mainstay environmentalists, Ralph Nader managed to turn the Green Party into the Gangrene Party. While the status of the Green Party is in doubt, the overall 2000 election results confirm that the environment and issues surrounding the environment are now part of mainstay American politics . . . no longer limited to fringe parties or candidates. In fact, in a wide-ranging April 2000 survey by the Gallup Organization, only the civil rights (85 percent) and women's rights movement (82 percent) topped the environmental movement (78 percent) in social importance to the American public.[35]

If there is mainstream acceptance of the importance of the environment and if most of us do see a direct connection to the economy, how deep does this linkage awareness go? With this question in mind, I dug again into more poll results. I found this most revealing opinion statistic from 1992. In a poll for TIME/CNN, 1,400 adults were asked:

> "Will the government's current environmental regulations weaken or strengthen the economy in the long run?"
> The response: Weaken 23 percent
>   Strengthen 27 percent
>   No Effect 36 percent[36]

What makes this response significant is not the 27 percent who said "strengthen," but the fact that more people saw a positive instead of a negative connection between environmental regulation and economic health. This revelation about government regulation suggests to me that the linkage connection runs deeper than just election-time awareness of issues.

Along this same line of polling is a tracking, bellwether question which Wirthlin Worldwide asks every year. They ask, "Do you agree that environmental standards cannot be too high and that continuing improvements must be made regardless of costs?" Here is the track record on those agreeing.

ENVIRONMENTALISM BAROMETER
"ENVIRONMENTAL STANDARDS CANNOT BE TOO HIGH, AND CONTINUING IMPROVEMENTS MUST BE MADE REGARDLESS OF COST"

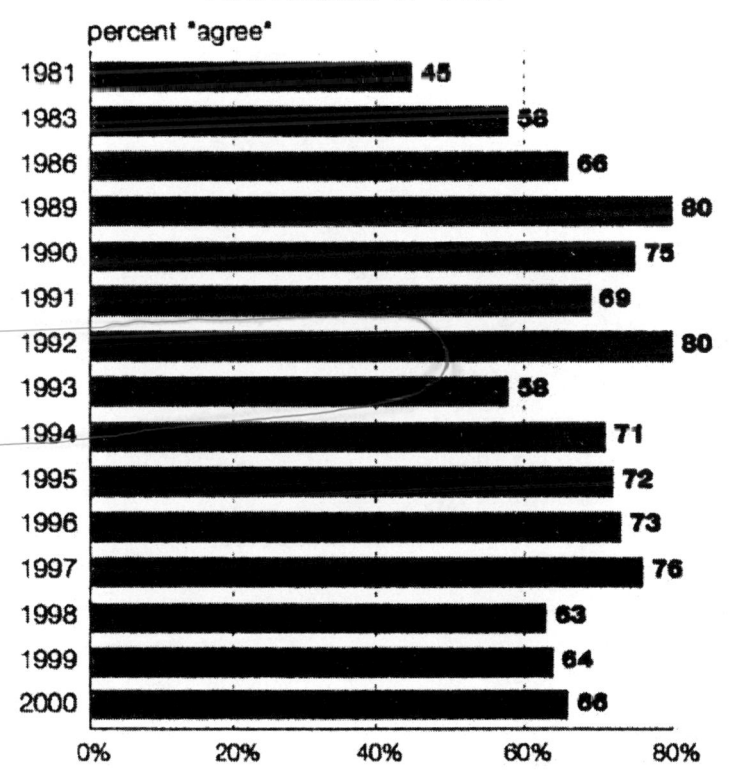

percent "agree"

Year	%
1981	45
1983	58
1986	66
1989	80
1990	75
1991	69
1992	80
1993	58
1994	71
1995	72
1996	73
1997	76
1998	63
1999	64
2000	66

As noted by the graph, in 2000, 66 percent agreed, down from a five-year high of 76 percent in 1997.[37] Had I known about this survey back in 1992, I would have challenged at least one anti-environment speaker at the Prosperity and Protection Conference.

This ability of Americans to see the environment and the economy as hand in hand is perhaps a function of most Americans simply being pro-environment. A 1995 Gallup poll reported that roughly two-thirds of Americans considered themselves to be "environmentalists".[38] The Wirthlin Group found in 1999 that 66 percent of Americans consider themselves active environmentalists (10 percent) or sympathetic to environmental concerns (56 percent).[39] Three in four people take time at home to recycle cans, bottles or paper.[40] Within this majority there are subgroups that have stronger feelings about the environment than other groups. Based on demographic analysis of their study results, Wirthlin Worldwide reports:

- Women are more concerned about the environment than men
- Young people are more concerned about the environment than older people
- People who have not graduated from college are more concerned about the environment than those who have completed college.
- Democrats and Independents are more concerned about the environment than Republicans.[41]

It is the third bullet that surprises me. I definitely thought that concern for the environment was associated with a college education.

Next, I wondered what survey results aimed at setting the economy against the environment tell us. The CNN exit polls for Election 2000 asked voters: Which is more important, economic growth or the environment? Forty-eight percent said that economic growth is more important than the environment, leaving 46 percent saying the opposite.[42] This equal divide confirms for me that a vast majority of Americans value both. Take, for example, the results of the Harris Feel-Good Index. Sixty-nine percent of Americans feel good about the quality of the air, water and environment where they live and work. An equal amount feels good about the nation's economy.[43] No wonder most Americans do not want to choose between the environment and the economy. Why choose between things you feel good about if you don't have to? We all want to continue "feeling good" about the environment and the economy and we're equally divided when forced to answer one way or the other.

In the final analysis, it doesn't matter which is more important, because we want and need both. Fourth-generation logger George Atiyeh from Oregon recognizes that he needs a healthy environment as well as a job. "Rural communities will have to adapt or die," says Atiyeh. "It isn't Norman Rockwell out here anymore. Protecting the environment is something we all have to do."[44]

Don Judge, Executive Secretary of the Montana AFL/CEO, is critical of the environmental movement along similar lines. "I think the environmental movement has mishandled the issues tremendously," he says. "A long time ago, they should have focused on a responsible development plan—a responsible balance between local communities and local economies as opposed to the extremes of 'log it all or lock it up.'"[45]

Jon Roush, President of the Wilderness Society agrees and sees the bigger picture: "We need sustainable economies and sustainable conservation. The two are inseparable. We need to find ways to conserve the Earth's biological diversity without economic hardship. If we don't, neither nature nor people will flourish."[46]

A logger from Wrangell, Alaska said it all for me at a regional conference of municipalities and business. "You're looking at 'Mister In the Middle.' I'm a logger who cares about the environment, so I go to a meeting of environmentalists and they look at me like 'what the hell are you doing here'? Then I go to a meeting at the mill and if I don't buy the company line 100 percent, they treat me like I'm all painted green. This is nonsense. I am not the enemy. I am part of the solution, but there is no place for me."

We need a place not only for the displaced logger, but also for the seven out of ten Americans who believe that economic development and environmental protection go hand in hand. In the interest of providing such a place, I offer this first principle of eco-nomics:

Eco-nomic Principle No. 1
Conservation Is a Universal Value

Equality, justice, and freedom are core values of Americans. While we may disagree as to the application of these values in particular circumstances, we agree that these are shared values among our neighbors. It is time to recognize that after decades of inspirational writing from Thoreau to John Muir, after a half-century of national leadership from Theodore Roosevelt to Al Gore, and after the 1970s sweep of environmental laws, conservation is also a core value of most Americans. The desire for conservation is no longer confined to *Field and Stream* readers, to viewers of PBS "Nature" and to LL Bean shoppers. We all want the same thing—a job and the ability to raise a family in a clean and healthy environment. After all, two-thirds of most Americans consider themselves an environmentalist.

If you wonder about the validity of this principle, take a look again at how many Americans think environmental standards cannot be too high (see chart on page 34). To agree with this idea, a strong conservation value must be present. In April 2000 a Gallup poll revealed that 67 percent feel that protection of the environment should be given priority, even at the risk of curbing economic growth.[47] Voters today send the same message to President George W. Bush. A *Los Angeles Times* poll in May 2001 showed that a majority of Americans do not believe President Bush should sacrifice the environment for the economy or new energy production.[48]

Why do Americans feel this strongly? American history suggests it's because of our romantic attachment to the land. Historian G.F. White points out that our attitude toward planet Earth has evolved rapidly with the development of ideas and knowledge during the twentieth century. In his article, "Reflection on Changing Perceptions of the Earth," he suggests that four distinct views of the Earth can be noticed:

1) *Earth Surveyed* (circa 1920s)—The planet at this time was examined with human development in mind. Resources were seen as being unlimited and were viewed primarily for their potential use.
2) *Earth Developed*—Early surveys suggested that vast quantities of resources were waiting for development for human needs. Management schemes were advanced to both protect and develop resources. Some of these schemes involved mammoth development efforts.
3) *Earth at Risk*—The enthusiasm for development was met with predictions of an impending environmental crisis. Individuals noted that development was having some immediate unfavorable effects on natural and social systems. Visionaries also suggested that development efforts may produce some long-term effects as yet not perceivable.
4) *Earth as Spiritual Home*—Academics and political leaders are now recognizing the magnitude of global problems associated with development. As a result of this awaking, humans are being asked to view this planet as our finite home. This new perception recognizes the need to work in harmony with natural systems and the need to adopt sustainable visions of development.[49]

Our attitudes are shifting in the right direction. Conservation is part and parcel to our viewing Earth at Risk. If we are to collectively arrive at the fourth view of "Earth as Spiritual Home", we have no choice but to accept conservation as more than an ideal. We must accept conservation as a growing, universal value; as a value that can override the war zone rhetoric... rhetoric that we will continue to hear from the national pulpit and from the Hanks and Judiths in our towns. However, in the long run, values trump rhetoric.

CHAPTER 3

The Schooling Effect of Fish Politics

When your name is Troll in Alaska, it's synonymous with "Fish and Fishing." "You know, Troll, T-R-O-L-L, as in fishing for salmon off the back of your boat," I explain while placing a mail order. But many Alaskans also know the name Troll in association with either "fish art" or "fish politics." My brother Ray Troll, the Gary Larson of fish, entwines witty fish humor with art and science. Ray is the fish artist and I am the fish politician. In our own ways, we understand the schooling effect of fish. Ray in the scientific and artistic way; me in the way of fishermen and the communities they support. So Troll and fish go together just like salmon and school go together... at least up here in Alaska they do. After more than 20 years of living close to the pulse of fish, I've come to appreciate the cohesiveness of schooling salmon despite the divisiveness of salmon politics.

Visualize a vibrating school of salmon migrating 1,500 miles north and west through the plankton-rich waters of the Pacific. Visualize stocks of salmon merging together en masse, riding the currents of the emerald sea, hurriedly seeking their stream of origin like evening commuters in L.A. Of course, for salmon it's their only trip home. And what a triumphant trip home it is! Visualize the magnetism of coming together, of schooling like salmon. This image transfers over into political arena, particularly in Alaska where the industry spawned by these schools is as immense as the run, sometimes as high as 200 million returning salmon. And the more immense the industry, the more intense the politics.

When thousands of commercial fishermen and seafood processors from more than 2,000 miles of coastline come together and voice their concerns on political issues, they can be quite a positive force. The coming together, the creation of one loud voice for the industry of fish contributes to the greater good of fusing the agendas of the environment and the economy.

Every professional commercial fisherman has his future anchored to sustainable fisheries and habitat protection like a boat tied to the docks. The same relationship exists for the guided sport-fishing industry blossoming throughout the West. And like commercial fishing, the bigger the economic contribution, the stronger the pull can be for sustainable fisheries and habitat protection.[50] Recreational fishing now contributes $100 billion a year to the U.S. economy, including nearly $10 billion in direct expenditures on the West Coast alone. "With this economic [news] in hand, conservationists can now argue for both fish and jobs," notes Bill Shedd, chair of the American Sportfishing Association. Just like the schooling of fish, the coming together of fishermen—subsistence, sport and commercial—can be an awesome display of power and rejuvenation. I call this biological and political display, the "pull of fish."

While many Alaskans feel this "pull of fish," it is not confined to Alaska. The sustainable connection happens wherever there are fishermen who understand their ecological roots. Here's a synopsis of some stewardship standouts from the fishing industry in California, Texas and Maine.

California—Overall Fishing Industry

Stewardship Goal: To form a coalition of sport fishermen, commercial fishermen, environmentalists and 20 scientists in an effort to support a bill that shifts control of commercial fisheries management away the political arena (legislature) to the realm of science (Department of Fish and Game).

Result: A broad fishing coalition was formed resulting in a

successful lobbying campaign to sign into law the Marine Life Management Act. According to the Center for Marine Conservation, this bill is "probably the most significant advance in fisheries management and conservation for California in 50 years."[51]

Maine—Herring Industry

Stewardship Goal: To privately fund herring stock assessment research after many years of scientific negligence by government research institutions.

Result: Herring research is initiated and paid for by the industry. Subsequently, the rich reproductive areas for herring have been better identified, and now routine biological surveys are incorporated into fisheries management. Jeff Kaelin of the Maine Sardine Council sums up the experience of industry funding science this way, "Regulators and academics are eager to help fishermen help themselves and their fisheries. In the big picture our interests are identical."[52]

Texas—Shrimp Industry

Stewardship Goal: Be proactive and protect the reproductive habitat of endangered sea turtles and coordinate volunteer hatching efforts.

Results: Kick-started a 20-year-old turtle restoration project by unearthing turtle nests, transporting the eggs to hatching "corrals" and then releasing 18,000 turtle hatchlings back to the sea. Upon visiting the release site, officials from the National Marine Fisheries Services commented, "Anytime industry gets behind an environmental project like this we know it will succeed."[53]

Back to Alaska's fishing industry. In chapter one, I explained how I, as a representative of the fishing industry, cast an eco-nomic vision into the Tongass Timber Reform Act debate. While the battle over timber reforms played out in the Washington, DC arena, there was a similar battle being played out at the state level in regard to forest practices on state and private lands in the Tongass. The fundamental issue was the same—how to properly allow for logging while protecting other forest resources. This is a story of conflict resolution between the environmental community and the timber industry built on the bridge provided by the fishing industry. This local success story about the Tongass highlights two eco-nomic principles.

About 400,000 acres of commercial timber in the Tongass lies in the hands of native corporations. Rather than create a reservation system, Alaska Natives chose a different route of settling native claims. In exchange for relinquishing claims to territorial land and allowing the Alaska Oil Pipeline to go through, Congress deeded 44 million acres of land, granted 1 billion dollars to Alaska Natives and established 13 regional corporations and 203 village corporations. One of these regional corporations and 9 village corporations inherited a vast wealth of old-growth forests—32 percent of the entire commercial forestlands in the Tongass. This was truly a forest prize to be converted into jobs and dividends for native shareholders.

Logging on native land commenced in great earnest in the early 1980s. The only tool to guide the harvesting of timber was a long-on-intent and short-on-specifics 1979 Forest Resources and Practices Act, which required only minimal streamside or habitat protection. The act was written when the notion of a private timber base was just a twinkle in Alaska's adolescent eyes. With such a weak act, the native corporation lands were being logged aggressively. It was not uncommon to find bank-to-bank streamside clear-cutting and multiple cutting entries in the same watershed over a short time span, i.e. logging the wrong way. But timber jobs were now appearing in villages that previously depended solely on commercial fishing. Dividend checks began to flow to thousands of Tlingit and Haida Indians. The riches of the forest were flowing in new ways to those most in need.

By the mid-to-late 1980s, the degradation to salmon streams was too much for commercial fishermen to look the other way. Native fishermen began to raise the issue of habitat protection within their own shareholders' meetings; they began to join the chorus of similarly concerned commercial fishermen who were raising the issue in community forums. With the elders of the fleet and the elders of the native community beginning to speak out, a potent voice for change emerged. At the center of this merger was an Angoon fishermen named Dennis Eames. Dennis, with his jet-black hair, appeared to be an Alaska Native, but he was not. He had married into village life on Admiralty Island. Dennis, being a perennial highliner of the fleet, simultaneously became an economic mainstay for the village of Angoon. He also became president of one of Southeast Alaska's largest and most influential fishing organizations—Southeast Alaska Seiners. Dennis' potent voice echoed the growing call for change:

> "We get two kinds of checks in my family, one from the processor and one from Kootznoowoo's timber operations. I want to keep it that way, but it won't stay that way if we keep logging down to the salmon streams. I don't overfish. But doing my part to make sure enough salmon reach the stream for spawning does little good if logging smothers the eggs in silt from runoff or if the salmon cook in unshaded streams. Fishermen understand about doing their part to ensure the return of salmon runs but we can't make it work by ourselves. We're all in this forest together. And as a fisherman who gets a dividend check from timber receipts, I want to see the timber industry do their part. I don't want a bigger dividend at the expense of my fish ticket."[54]

This message was echoed in the boardrooms of other native corporations. Sensing the opportunity, three fishing organizations of Southeast Alaska began to call for a formal review of the State Forest Resources and Practices Act. In response to the growing criticism and in recognition of the need to maintain a viable timber industry, Governor Steve Cowper set up a formal process to review the act. The Governor directed a consensus process overseen by a Steering Committee comprised of 5 representatives of forest owners and operators, 5 representatives of users of resources affected by forest practices (fishing and environmental groups) and 3 representatives from the state resource agencies. Recommendations for legislative changes would then be submitted to the 1990 Legislature at the request of the Governor.

Dennis Eames, now a member of the Steering Committee, walked into the Forest Practices Review Forum with high hopes and strong feelings. The Governor had altered the stage setting from one of conflict to one of potential resolution; now it was up to each Steering Committee member to make it work and not sell out in the process. However, Dennis walked into a charged atmosphere of the environmental community "feeling its oats" and the timber owners, the native corporations, threatening to pull out if this effort was going to result in a big financial hit to the industry. Shaking his head in disgust at the rhetoric replay, Dennis raised his hand to speak:

> "I'd much rather be working on my boat right now. The salmon season's done but I need to gear-up for black cod. Instead I'm here. I'm here because I care about our salmon streams. Salmon is my livelihood and the lifeblood of my village. I'm no biologist, but I see what's going on and I know we can't keep logging these corporation lands right down to the stream. That's why I'm here. I'm not here on any environmental mission to put another industry out of business. I'll have no part in such an effort. The communities of Southeast need a viable timber industry. But I am not about to waste my time here if every time we ask for a new way of logging, I hear a threat of walking out. I don't like making sets for salmon when the tide and current are all wrong; it's a waste of time. And I think that's what's beginning

to happen here. So we need to get down to some basic principles of what this forum is all about—things like *no big hit* to timber or fish—get the tide working with us not against us."[55]

The Steering Committee, with the aid of professional mediators, then began talking about principles necessary for any system that would balance the need of all the resources at stake. After considerable deliberations, the Steering Committee adopted these guiding principles:

1. Fairness. Any successful system must be based on shared risk and incentive for both timber owners and regulators to make it work.
2. No "Big Hit." Neither fish nor timber should bear an inordinate share of the burden; that a balance must be found. No private landowner should have to bear an unusually large burden.
3. Enforceable. Standards and regulations should be understandable and measurable for ease in implementation.
4. Professional Management. To provide optimum utilization of manpower and some system flexibility for fish and water quality protection, and timber management, the new system would require careful planning and targeted field effort.[56]

With these principles in hand, the working groups of biologists and stakeholders set up a series of negotiation sessions on each major aspect of forest practices—from road building to enforcement. Recognizing that streamside protection and water quality was the heart of any meaningful reform to forest practices, the Steering Committee dealt with this aspect first.

Industry invoked the "no big hit" principle every time a no-harvest leave strip of timber (buffer) along certain stream types would get proposed. The best of the forest for fish is also the best of the forest for timber. Most salmon-spawning habitat is located in streams with flat gradients along valley bottoms. These salmon areas tend to have better drained soils that support high-quality and high-volume timber. Fortunately, this "no big hit" principle worked both ways. To counter the value of standing timber, fishing interests cited the value of coho salmon production over the 100-year rotation cycle. In 1985, the net value of a board foot of riparian timber returned $2.19 in coho salmon production and $1.25 in timber production. The economics of salmon production gave resource protection a more quantifiable, tangible value. Seeing the fish in the trees as well as the board foot value in the trees kept the debate on equal terms instead of allowing it to deteriorate into the standard jobs versus environment battle. More than any other principle, the "no big hit" principle kept the negotiations moving toward a fair conclusion on streamside buffers.

In June 1989, all affected interest groups signed a comprehensive, 67-page agreement-in-principle. The pivotal part of the agreement included a streamside protection zone that required a 100-foot, no-cut buffer strip along all salmon streams on state forestlands. A lesser buffer (66 feet) was designated on salmon streams within private lands. Allowances were made for limited harvest within the buffer on private lands, provided that riparian habitat was protected as determined on a case-by-case basis with concurrence from the Alaska Department of Fish and Game.

With the "heart of the matter" agreed upon, the negotiations on other aspects of forest practice such as reforestation, road construction, and timber sale notification fell into place. In 1990 the Alaska Legislature passed the Alaska State Forest Practices Act to the cheers of the environmental, fishing and timber communities for it was the first time that any legislation made it through both the House and Senate Chambers without a single amendment. The timber industry and the environmental community publicly acknowledged the unique contributions made by the fishing industry in the course of the negotiations.

Since its passage in 1990, Alaska's Forest Practices Act has been called the best in the nation by policy makers and the timber industry. In 1996, the Board of Forestry (comprised of representatives similar to the Steering Committee) convened a team of scientists to review the field data to see if the Act was working as intended to protect fish, wildlife and water quality. The scientific and technical review found that the Act was fundamentally sound; that it was basically working as intended. However, the review team also found numerous areas where the Act could be improved to the benefit of all users, such as correctly interpreting when a natural barrier to salmon passage existed. Like all resource management efforts, the Forest Practices Act needed to evolve.

Once again representing the salmon industry, I found myself serving on a committee with timber and environmental interests. The charge was to come to agreement on the regulatory changes needed to retool the State Forest Practices Act. I was pleased to play a pivotal role in crafting a workable and meaningful agreement. For the second time in Alaska's legislative history, a resource management bill passed amendment free on the strength of a negotiated agreement among vested interests. These forest/fish experiences have shown me that vested interest can work to protect resources as well as promote industry viability.

Following the fish and following the fishermen leads me to:

Eco-nomic Principle No. 2
Invest in "Ecologically Tuned In" Vested Interest

All renewable resource industries have a vested interest in the sustainability of the raw resource, such as timber, fish, and land. Some industries act responsibly in protecting this interest, others do not due to short-term perspectives or lack of vision. Acting responsibly means an industry recognizes their ecological roots and promotes appropriate environmental protection. These industries see that the environmental and economic agenda of resource politics can be one and the same, period. Privatization of access to public resources can lead to a stronger connection to the resource base and if designed correctly a stronger tie to environmental protection. When the ecological and economic connection is made, vested interest can work to protect as well as to promote.

This connection to vested interests is not new, nor is it limited to fishermen. Nowadays, there are responsible, "tuned in" ranchers, loggers, and farmers, and a global industry surrounding ecotourism. The connection occurs in many places. The words of Buzz Eades, a Northwest logger, show this connection:

> "There are hundreds of people like me that have a feeling for this land, and a feeling for responsibility about the stewardship of the land. We live, work and play here. I think we probably have a better feel for how to take care of this land than the people who come here once a year to vacation."[57]

This connection of vested interests is also apparent in the well-established school of thought called free market environmentalism. Free market environmentalism starts from the self-interests embodied in private ownership. By assigning private rights in the commons, property owners have an economic reason to protect the commons.[58]

Capitalism is based on a system of markets and private property rights. According to the authors of *Eco-Sanity*, when rights are correctly defined and enforced, capitalism will protect the environment because:

- It creates incentives to do the right things,
- It generates and distributes needed information,
- It enables people to trade things or rights in order to solve problems that otherwise can't be solved;[59]

The owner of a resource stands to benefit if the resource is put to its best use and managed for sustainability. Conversely, the owner will suffer a loss if the resource is misused or squandered. If the property right is transferable, the owner must consider not only the value they place on a resource, but also the values that others may place on it.[60] If this resource is abused and unhealthy then it will not be valued as well by other prospective owners. Getting this value connection in the marketplace provides an inherent incentive to do right by the resource.

The traditional adversarial relationship between a regulated resource user and regulator dissipates over time as the interest of doing "right by the resource" becomes a mutual interest. Often the resource user is the first to observe change in the character of the resource. Sharing this information with resource managers enhances their ability to manage wisely. Similarly, resource managers are more apt to seek observational data to correlate or validate their professional hunches when the regulated resource user remains approachable.

A market system allows disagreements over the value of natural resources to be resolved through the exchange of money or rights. Cooperation is possible in new ways when there are private, transferable rights. For example, the Audubon Society, a group opposed to oil and gas development in most wilderness settings, acted differently when it owned the land and mineral rights. Audubon's Rainey Wildlife Sanctuary in Louisiana is home to deer, otter, mink, thousands of geese and many other birds, yet since the 1960s it has been home to oil wells. In return for allowing Consolidated Oil and Gas to produce on the sanctuary, Audubon receives royalties. However, Audubon has imposed tough contractual restrictions on how the gas can be extracted. As a result of these restrictions, Audubon receives lower royalties. That is the price they paid for caring for the environment—all while allowing development to proceed.[61]

This example shows that the concept of vested interests protecting the environment is not limited to fishermen or ranchers. It just takes new ways of thinking to make the particular situation work for both the environmental and economic interests. Each side must understand that cooperation is sustained by self-interest. Having the right setting and forum makes a difference in being able to see these mutual self-interests and in turn allowing for these new perceptions to emerge. For example, the success of the Forest Practices story has much to do with changing the venue away from "slugging it out in the legislature" to a "try and work this out" setting. The leadership shown by Governor Cowper in appointing a Stakeholders Steering Committee and in hiring a neutral (non-agency) facilitator for extended work sessions highlights this principle:

Eco-nomic Principle No. 3
Provide a Forum to Advocate Balance

The existing public process of "release a document and hold a public hearing" does not provide a forum for seeking balanced solutions or politically achievable compromises. Work sessions and informal conferences should be favored over the 5-minute "state your name for the record" drill. Public hearings are suitable for advocacy but not for conflict resolution. Any political advocate worth their salary will loyally spend their 5 minutes of public hearing time advocating their organizational or business interest, not waste their allotted time on finding balance. Whenever possible, convene roundtable discussions. The convener of work sessions or roundtable discussions should be perceived as neutral and as a professional whose purpose is to be a neutral facilitator. This often excludes government agencies as neutral conveners. When this is recognized, then the agency host actively participates and pays for the professional services. The time, setting and forum for public involvement must change if one wants open dialogue on ways to find balance. Give people a chance to check their advocacy at the door and talk as problem solvers. Once a conducive setting has been found, recognize that seeking common ground does not make one any less a conservationist or a development advocate.

CHAPTER 4

Sharing the Sound Responsibly

This is the story of the might-have-never-been disaster of the *Exxon Valdez* oil spill of 1989. In 1989, we all paid the price for letting industry and government ignore other vested interests. The most powerful resource extraction industry in the world—the oil industry, discounted the interests and knowledge of Alaska's fishing industry. The resulting tragedy proved costly in many ways.

The *Exxon Valdez* was one of a dozens of tankers transporting crude oil—at the rate of three or four a day—from the end of the Alyeska pipeline at Valdez, through Prince William Sound and the Gulf of Alaska to the refineries of the world. In the early 1970s, the commercial fishermen of Prince William Sound had opposed the pipeline to saltwater at Valdez. This would require transport of the potentially lethal cargo through some of the richest salmon grounds in the world. The fishermen argued that crude oil in a pipeline or a tanker is not poisonous, but crude oil in the water is deadly. A small voice in the world of global business, the fishermen lost the fight for the Alaska-Canada route even with the help of State Representative Jay Hammond (see chapter nine). The pipeline from Prudhoe Bay to the port of Valdez was built. The interests of commercial fishing—which were also the interests of the marine ecosystem—were thought to be the lesser interests, and were therefore largely ignored.

Let's look at the problems caused by failing to listen to ecologically connected interests before, during and after the tanker disgorged 11 million gallons of crude oil into Prince William Sound.

We'll examine it through the eyes of my friend Riki Ott, whose name and character resemble a cunning, energized sea otter. She delivers habitat advocacy with the same zeal as an otter diving and feasting on a sea urchin bed—zeal that led Riki to become known as the Sibyl of the Sound. Just like a Greek Sibyl who foretold the future, Riki warned the Valdez City Council about the likelihood of a major spill just six hours before the *Exxon Valdez* hit the reef.[62]

Before the Spill

Having completed her marine biology doctorate in sediment toxicology, Riki Ott sought a real world respite—commercial fishing in Alaska. "Commercial fishing made me realize that environmentalism isn't a separate entity unto itself," declares Riki, "that it's linked with economics and the social need of people." After two years of gillnetting Copper River Reds, Riki decided it was time to volunteer for Cordova District Fishermen United (CDFU), the local fishing organization. The oldest commercial fishermen's organization in the state of Alaska, CDFU led the losing battle for the Alaska-Canada pipeline route in the 70s.

In the fall of 1987, Riki attended the CDFU board meeting, where oil is but one of several issues on the table. Upon entering the meeting, Riki sensed a rising wave of concern and awaited her time to speak. Toward the end of the meeting, she offered to help work the Alyeska Pipeline issue.

"We've got plenty of issues, why cut your teeth on Alyeska?" asked Bob Blake, the seasoned board President. Other fishermen shrugged in disbelief that anyone would volunteer for such a difficult issue.

"Because I have a doctorate in sediment toxicology from the University of Washington, specializing in oil," responded Riki. Expressions of doubt soon changed to expressions of amazed relief. Blake then jumped on the opportunity for CDFU to gain scientific credibility and moved to appoint Riki to the Board of Directors.

She was accepted unanimously. Blake then passed a five-inch pile of paper to Riki stating, "here's the National Pollution Discharge Elimination System Permit (NPDES) for the oil terminal. We know they are polluting. We just don't know how they're doing it. Plus every time we go over to talk with Alyeska we can't get past the lawyers. It's a stonewall. Here, read these and tell us where you think about Alyeska polluting. The hearing is on Wednesday."

Riki accepted the pile and immersed herself in paper. The Riki Ott that many Alaskans know as an environmental jet fighter was launched into the world of oil and fish politics. Riki's energies and environmental values were now focused sharply on one issue, like a mother otter protecting her pup from danger.

Riki, as a scientific expert, empowered through the credibility of industry upstaged the NPDES public hearing. It was not a slam-dunk approval of the permit application. She was warned by one government scientist, "Watch your back side, you have the credentials to discredit the oil industry scientists." This warning only challenged her more.

Discovering that the ballast treatment facility was sloppily operated, she began to wonder about the tanker operation and oil spill contingency plans. It didn't take much for her suspicions to be aroused. If the ballast water operations were being so sloppily managed, so too, could be the tanker safety operations. "Forget chronic pollution from ballast water, we're going to have a major spill here and not be ready for it," Riki informed CDFU. With more research into the availability of spill containment boom, she confirmed her suspicions. The next challenge was to hone her message and get it delivered without being marginalized as some wing-nut environmentalist.

Riki took to speech writing for local classrooms and Rotary meetings. Her first talk, "Beyond Foul Nests," focused on the role of oil in the marine ecosystem. An interesting talk but not action motivating. Next, she opted to highlight the potential economic impact to the fishing industry and the community. This talk included a new angle—the economic implications of a big spill for the commercial fishing industry.

The new speech, "Spilled Oil and the Alaska Fishing Industry," was well received in Cordova, but it didn't go very far in Washington D.C., where the fishermen had sent Riki to make the rounds with resource congressmen. "No one likes to hear about potential problems in D.C.," noted Riki. "They only want to hear about real problems."

Gaining headway in Cordova, Riki then set her sights on trying to wake up the community of Valdez, the bastion of Alaska oil. A few days before a regularly scheduled Valdez City Council meeting, she received a call from the mayor of Valdez asking, "Can you pinch-hit for a canceled speaker and talk about tanker safety and risks to the community?" Riki agreed. The scheduled speaker from Alyeska Pipeline Company had to attend a company gathering in celebration of safe transport of oil. No such conflict for Riki. She arranged to fly to Valdez, but bad weather kept her grounded in Cordova and she had to give her speech by telephone, warning that a major spill was highly possible. Judging by the questions after her talk, Riki realized that she had made an impression.

Six hours after Riki's talk, the *Exxon Valdez* rammed onto Bligh Reef, a well-marked rock five miles outside the obstacle course of Valdez Narrows. The news "Tanker on the Rocks!" stunned and horrified the residents of Cordova and Valdez. Lifelong fishermen who fought the pipeline were too heartsick to say "I told you so." Before long the whole nation was equally shocked, as the footage of oil-covered otters splashed across primetime news. The *Exxon Valdez* story brought the media to Alaska like the Superbowl does to New Orleans. The nation grieved at the sight of this ecological tragedy.

Looking back, Riki offers these comments:

> "In my talks to the city councils, I was not saying 'No' to oil. I was saying can't we get more prevention and spill containment equipment in here because otherwise it's going to hurt us all economically. Scientists from both government and industry were coming to me in private and lending my message support. I was not being marginalized as a radical. I was starting to be listened to."

During the Spill

Day one—Riki, like every local resident, was glued to the radio. Commercial fishermen in agonized disbelief attended the morning briefings held by Exxon and the Coast Guard. The water remained calm as millions of gallons of crude oil spread about from the grounded tanker. Yet the oil industry took no immediate action to contain or pick up the spilled oil. Tempers flared and finger pointing began. U.S. Representatives and Senators called Riki to say, "Please come and testify before my committee."

Day two of the spill—Cordova fishermen realized that the crisis called for action. They could not stand by the poor, ineffective response of the oil industry. Incredulous reporters began to realize that the oil company consortium in charge of the pipeline had subverted its responsibility to prevent spills. The individual oil shippers had neither the intention nor the equipment to contain a large, spreading spill.

Swinging into action, fishermen worked the phones to locate any available oil boom anywhere in the world. Bucket brigades and herring pumps were put into full service. At least a little oil was being sucked up now. A midnight truck scheme, put together by one entrepreneurial fisherman, brought down "Super Soakers" boom from the North Slope. With boom arriving by plane, fishing boats signed up as oil clean-up vessels.

Day three—Fishermen began to deploy boom in sensitive areas and near hatcheries. The oil companies finally managed to locate additional boom.

Day four—A crippling storm blasted in. Nature worked on her own to breakup and disperse the oil. The prevailing currents and wind drove oil onto the beaches throughout the spill's spreading path across Prince William Sound. Eventually the spill spread as far as Cook Inlet and Kodiak Island. Riki was now stashed away from spill logistics. At the direction of fellow fishermen, she was confined in a room to record the events for soon-to-follow Congressional hearings.

The nation grieved at the nightly news images of oiled, lifeless otters, of eyeless carcasses of seabirds, and of local residents crying at the sight of their fouled nest. Citizens across the country clamored for government response. As the story of events leading up to and during the spill unfolded, the credibility of Riki and commercial fishermen soared fast. The problem of oil spill preparedness was no longer a potential problem. It was there and it was devastating. Exxon Corporation kicked in millions of dollars for an oil spill clean-up effort and the rebuilding of their public image. Americans watched images of workers clad in oil-smeared raingear using diapers to wipe rocks.

Post Oil Spill

At the end of the four months of clean-up efforts, Exxon had spent over $3 billion. Active listening began by once passive Congressmen. The fishermen's testimony eventually led to fundamental changes in disaster liability law. Congress quickly passed out the Oil Prevention Act of 1990, mandating double hull tankers. Citizens oversight committees became the rule across the nation. Exxon Corporation also paid the U.S. government and the state of Alaska a total of $500 million for the remediation, restoration and recovery of the Sound. The sense of emergency amidst a flood of grief for the Sound made the *Exxon Valdez* a milestone in raising America's environmental awareness and sense of responsibility.

Unfortunately, Exxon's sense of responsibility did not extend to the fishermen of the oiled waters. Ten plus years later, they still await the $5 billion dollars awarded to them in civil litigation. Nonetheless, the *Exxon Valdez* oil spill is an important chapter in our collective societal consciousness that we must remain ever diligent in meeting our environmental responsibilities.

Ten years later it is safe to say that the Sound is on the path to ecological recovery in some important ways, although it's still too soon to say much about the long-term chronic effects of petrochemicals. Regardless, the spill should not have occurred. The spill's immediate devastation of marine life remains a disaster in the ecological record books. The lives of fishermen and communities have been changed forever. It is appropriate to ask, "What would have happened if commercial fishermen were listened to earlier? Would the spill have occurred? If yes, would it have been any different?

An independent analysis prepared for Congress by the U.S. Coast Guard in May 1998 concluded, if the *Exxon Valdez* tanker had a double hull as originally promised to the Cordova fishermen, the spill would still have occurred. The inner hull would likely have been punctured, given the force of impact onto Bligh Reef, but the spill might have been 60-80 percent smaller. A spill 70 percent smaller—3.3 million gallons instead of 11 million gallons—would have made the fishing interests well worth listening to. Next, what if the radar system had been upgraded as requested by fishermen? Here we enter the "maybe not at all" scenario. A total of $8.3 billion (assuming Exxon complies with court rulings to pay punitive and compensatory damages to fishermen) should make the promise to fishermen well worth keeping . . . that is unless you're big enough like Exxon to just set aside $5 billion in a trust account for injured parties and recoup costs on interest earnings.

I like to think that the oil companies learned the most expensive lesson in those first awful hours after the spill. They learned they should have listened to the people who lived on the shores of the Sound and fished its waters. These fishermen knew about far more than just fish. They knew the currents, tides, and weather patterns better than anyone else. They knew how to assess preparedness. Their interests should have been reckoned with, but in the early spring of 1989, it became too late to go back. The only hope is that from tragedy comes transformation.

We now have more stringent requirements for tanker safety, response capability, and cleanup. Most importantly, the principle of reconciling economic and social interests between resource dependent industries and the public is now institutionalized in the creation of the Regional Citizens Advisory Councils (RCAC) for Prince William Sound, Cook Inlet and the Gulf of Alaska. Authorized by the Coast Guard and funded by the oil companies, these regional groups represent the interests of native Alaskans, environmentalists, local towns and commercial fishing in ensuring safe passage of oil.

Today, powerful tractor tugs escort loaded tankers out of the Sound. A world-class oil spill prevention and response system is in place. Fleets of fishing boats recruited and administered by CDFU are regularly trained and drilled as first responders. The oil consortium provides state-of-the-art response and clean-up vessels. Double-hull tankers are replacing single-hull tankers. Oil-producing nations from around the world are modeling their prevention and response practices after the system now in place in Alaska. Learning to share the sound responsibly is the transformation occurring from this tragedy. The before and after the oil spill events shed light on this principle:

Eco-nomic Principle No. 4
Compatibility Works

Like species sharing the same ecological niches, industries can share the same dependency on a healthy ecosystems. And similar to species, industries can find cooperative strategies that provide for mutual benefit. And as noted by Dr. E.P. Odum, who many view as the father of ecology, species diversity is directly correlated with ecosystem stability.[63] Similarly, communities relying on multiple resource dependent industries as opposed to a single extractive industry are economically more stable. Because the ecological base of one resource industry often overlaps into the base or area of another resource-dependent industry, seeking compatibility among resource industries can promote better management of that shared resource base. The web effect of shared economic and ecological systems makes seeking compatibility of resource-dependent industries a successful eco-nomic strategy. To ignore this web effect and not listen responsively to the needs of another resource-dependent industry can, as we know from the *Exxon Valdez* have dire, costly consequences.

To better understand the ecological subtleties of this principle, it is worth noting that negative and positive relations between populations of species eventually tend to balance one another if the ecosystem is to achieve any kind of stability.[64] Ecologist W.C. Allee (who wrote extensively about species interaction) believed that the beginnings of cooperation between species are found throughout nature and evolve from commensalisms (one population benefiting) to protocooperation (both populations benefiting) to mutualism (both populations benefiting and now dependent on each other).[65] And like diversity, species cooperation promotes stability within defined ecosystems.

Though man is all the same species, we place different sets of needs to the ecosystem. We also interact at different trophic levels i.e. sometimes we consume primary plant production and other times we consume secondary animal production or even detritus in the form of oil. The ecological needs of the farmer, the fishermen and the oilman are as different as moose, salmon and bear, and in this regard we are different populations sharing the same ecosystem and striving for stability.

This desire for stability extends into the economic world as well. Alaska's economy depends as much on oil as it does on renewable resource jobs. A study done by the University of Alaska's Institute of Social and Economic Research determined that jobs derived directly from natural resources (fishing, tourism, guiding, wildlife viewing, subsistence and resource management professionals) numbered 55,000. This is six times more than the 9,000 produced directly from the oil industries.[66] These figures confirm that in Alaska the foundation is there for this compatibility principle to work. And similarly so, a network of professions dependent on healthy ecosystems is likely to exist in many rural areas.

Several years later, I had the pleasure of reminding Riki of this compatibility principle; to use what she taught me through example. In 1997, Riki was serving as Habitat Committee Chair of United Fishermen of Alaska (UFA) and I was serving as Executive Director. The issue of concern was a legislative bill to roll back the state's water quality standards to accommodate the mining industry. Riki wanted to take the issue head on by engaging EPA, i.e. use the non-compliance regulatory hammer. I cautioned, "Riki, you're right on the technical and legal aspects that this bill would give EPA a green light to usurp the state's water quality program, but I just don't see that playing well with this anti-government legislature. Instead, let's appeal to their economic motives and push the fisheries-mining compatibility button. You taught me this with all your work on oil issues." It didn't take long for Riki to agree.

Here is how I played the economics of clean water and the need to promote compatibility between two of Alaska's resource industries. This is the short version:

"Dirty Water Bill" Threatens Alaska Fish Marketing

> The state of Alaska invests in and markets "pure" Alaska salmon from Alaska's pristine waters. Consumer confidence in Alaska seafood is driven by the perception that Alaska's fish are pure because Alaska's water is pure. Clean water means clean fish. Like many industries dealing with informed and concerned consumers, the Alaska Seafood Marketing Institute (ASMI) recognizes the economic advantages of Alaska's "clean" image in building consumer confidence. ASMI even includes government water quality surveys in their press packets.
>
> This "Dirty Water Bill" threatens the economic stability of our industry at a time when we must compete against farmed salmon on the basis of the consumer's perception of superior quality. UFA implores the Alaska legislature not to

> undermine our advantage in the 'economics of perception'—to keep Alaska's water quality standards strong.
>
> Despite its sponsors' intention to promote development, this legislation is sure to backfire.
>
> HB 51 would eliminate the requirements for multiple-use compatibility in the development of Alaska's water quality standards. The proposed law would set standards to accommodate the most degrading user at the expense of other water users. Multiple-use management is necessary for healthy statewide economic growth.
>
> Seafood—both harvesting and processing—is the state's largest source of private sector employment with 20,000 direct jobs. As important as mining is to Alaska, our industry, which is threatened by this bill, provides more than 13 times as many jobs as the mining industry. We believe in fostering economic development across all industries. Instead, HB 51 ill advisedly pits one industry against another.

This message got delivered repeatedly in the legislature and in media with fishermen from across the state weighing in with a similar message to their elected officials. The "Dirty Water Bill" languished and eventually died in committee. Fortunately, this was a relatively straightforward resolution. Applying this eco-nomic principle on larger, more complex issues requires some finesse and judgment.

CHAPTER 5

The Attraction of Lawsuit Avoidance

Whether the issue is grazing, logging or land development, the NIMBY (Not in My Back Yard) factor lurks like a land mine waiting to be triggered by a wayward foot. When a NIMBY land mine goes off, watch out for lawsuits coming. Whether it be NIMBY mines, liability traps or NEPA (National Environmental Policy Act) appeals, lawsuits are quickly becoming commonplace in many of our communities. To some, litigation is a tactic, not a result of failed negotiations. To many non-profit warriors wrapped in a worthy cause, litigation is the sword hidden beneath the cape ready to be unleashed with the first sign of non-compliance. Litigation as a tactic is certainly what I was taught when I took a course in Environmental Litigation from Yale School of Law in 1976.

In the early years of the environmental movement, litigation was an invaluable tool, which forced businesses to stop polluting and clean up the environment. The Clean Air and Water Acts were the first of their kind and the industry balked at regulation. Litigation by public interest groups soon became the desired, first recourse of action. But times are changing. And perhaps what was once good, necessary litigation in moderation is proving to be counterproductive in excess today. Steve Tachera, Executive Director of the Lake Tahoe Gaming Alliance thinks so:

> "In the '60s, '70s, and '80s the tourist industry and the environmental community fought long and bitter legal battles over development, and painful lessons were learned.

> Me suing you, you suing me. I mean, calling each other names and that, we did all that here and it's not worth a damn, I mean, it doesn't get you anywhere."[67]

The business and environmental community of Lake Tahoe learned about the poisonous nature of repetitive lawsuits the hard way. Fed up with the lawsuit barrage, the judge in the latest "banning new construction" lawsuit convinced the litigating parties to sit down and talk to each other. Representing the business community, Steve Tachera comments, "It was pretty interesting that there were ten issues that we could agree on and maybe one or two that we would disagree on. We agreed to set those aside and work for the ten."[68] From these meetings, the environmental community and business leaders discovered that they shared a common concern for protecting the splendor of Lake Tahoe. It was the *once* clear, blue water that made Tahoe stand out from other gambling resorts. Cleaning up the lake, making it clear, topped the list. After several years of directed recuperative attention, the lake now serves as a testament to the value of talking as an alternative to lawsuits. This chapter is about moving beyond the tactic; it's about important alternatives to lawsuits—mediation and community-based collaboration.

Through the decades, the Sierra-Nevada Mountain Range of California has seen many contentious issues from the Hetch Hetchy Dam to the Redwoods. From an area sown with legal conflicts, rises a budding example of collaboration. Today there exists the Sierra Nevada Alliance, a coalition of environmentalists, loggers, ranchers, and developers that has begun the process of breaking down years of distrust. Instead of prolonging the years of finger pointing and court battles the Sierra Nevada Alliance is, at the present, mostly about communication and understanding the other side's needs. Self-described "environmental wacko" and board member Linda Blum exemplifies this new dialogue:

> "We have a stake here. We're not trying to make this our playground, which is the stereotype that is very often applied

to us. This is our backyard; we live here. And we acknowledge that our neighbors also live here and want to make a living here, but we want to make sure that *it isn't just a working forest but it's a forest where everything still works.*"⁶⁹

A "working forest" in this context ties the community economically and ecologically. The Sierra Alliance and organizations like them generate dialogue on defining what constitutes a "working forest." They present an alternative to the lawsuit route. Unfortunately there are many areas where this bridge-building dialogue doesn't exist, and loggers and environmentalists remain gravely at odds with each other. In some communities, it is a chasm of polarity, and the opportunities for bridge building are scarce. Having lived in such communities, I know it's important to seize every bridge-building opportunity that pops up.

In Juneau, Alaska where I now live, the mining industry provides an example of the right way and the wrong way to go about bridge building between industry and the environmental community. Juneau is Alaska's capital city with a population of 30,000 people. It has a rich history of mining in the ore-laden mountains, so it's no surprise that in the 1990s two gold mining projects were being proposed at the same time. In 1987, Coeur Alaska began exploratory development of the Kensington Mine, 50 miles north of Juneau, while Echo Bay Mines began exploratory development of the A-J Mine, 3 miles south of Juneau. While the Echo Bay mine began the permitting process about a year ahead of Coeur Alaska, the timing and scale of the projects were close enough to examine and contrast the community approaches taken by each mining company.

These two mining projects presented an ideal case study for my class in Natural Resource Administration. What follows are excerpts that the involved parties shared with my University of Alaska class. To provide context for events that occurred outside of the class schedule, this summary also includes dialogue from follow-up interviews. Mr. Rick Richens with Coeur Alaska and Doug

Mertz, an environmental attorney, appeared together and shared these insights.

Coeur Alaska took the bridge-building approach to local and state permitting. "Mining doesn't have a real good track record," says Rick Richins, Coeur Alaska Mines vice-president of environmental affairs. "We recognized that and opted for sitting down with our critics to resolve our differences. While conflict resolution may be nothing new, the innovative part for us was having these discussions while our project was in the preliminary design stage. We talked when we were open and fluid to being responsive. This allowed us to integrate 'perspective mitigation' into project design."[70],[71]

For Coeur Alaska, the motivation for sitting down with local environmentalists and fishermen was lawsuit avoidance. Given a previous experience where an appeal on a simple monitoring and enforcement provision resulted in a delay cost of $2 million, Coeur was eager to approach the Alaska project differently. Coeur initiated dialogue early with the dominant environmental group—Southeast Alaska Conservation Council (SEACC). From these initial overtures, the concept of negotiating a Litigation Avoidance Agreement with the "Kensington Coalition" evolved.

The Kensington Coalition included the following members:
- Southeast Alaska Conservation Council (SEACC)
- Alaskans for Juneau—organized specifically to respond to mine proposals
- Juneau Audubon Society
- Taku Conservation Society—a member organization of SEACC
- Lynn Canal Conservation—a member organization of SEACC
- Haines Alaska Native Brotherhood and Sisterhood Camp 5
- United Fishermen of Alaska (UFA)
- United Southeast Alaska Gillnetters—a member organization of UFA

After receiving this background, a student asked, "What prompted this mix of environmental and fishing interests to sit at the same table with a poor track record industry? Why not just challenge the project as usual through the permit process?" Doug Mertz, an attorney representing the Kensington Coalition, answered bluntly, "Given agency cuts, turnover, and the political football atmosphere of the state and local governing bodies, we simply had no faith in public agencies to protect the public interest. As such, talking and working out concerns was a practical alternative for both parties."[72]

Contrary to Coeur Alaska, Echo Bay decided to flex the "We're Jobs" muscle in seeking permit authority to proceed. They did not engage in any pre-design dialogue on their project to reopen the historic AJ Mine abutting downtown Juneau. Instead they made lunchtime presentations to the Chamber of Commerce and the Rotary. They focused on supporters and the local planning authorities. They shunned the local environmental community: "Their [Echo Bay] company representatives expressed an attitude of 'we have nothing to talk to the environmental community about because we represent new jobs for the local economy and we'll just roll over the environmentalists,'" claims attorney Mertz.

A planning commission member who sat through numerous permit hearings on both mining projects sums up the different approaches this way. "It all boils down to whether the corporate culture recognizes that the National Environmental Policy Act is here to stay and treat environmental protection in the '90s as part of doing business. In one case, Coeur Alaska, the corporate culture was totally there. In the other case, Echo Bay, it was absent."

While an accepting attitude is one thing, action as we all know, is another matter. "Did Coeur respond to environmental concerns? What changed from the original development plan?" queried another student. Richens then passed out a newsletter detailing the changes made since the original plan.

The original plan involved a "wet tailing impoundment" with a 270-foot earthen dam designed to store 30 million tons of processed tailings. Tailings are the finely ground sand remaining after metal extraction. The original plan also called for on-site processing of the ore concentrate. The combined flotation and cyanide treated tailings were to be deposited behind the dam. Two major streams would have been diverted around the wet tailings impoundment to protect salmon populations. The original proposal also included discharge of treated effluent into a mixing zone in Lynn Canal, a scenic productive fjord of Southeast Alaska, with a mixing zone. A mixing zone is an area of water in which pollutants are allowed to exceed water quality standards before they are diluted by the receiving water body.

As a result of intense discussion, the design engineers reconfigured core concepts and developed an entirely new plan. According to Richens they made the following modifications:

- eliminated the need for cyanide by off-site processing of the flotation concentration.
- eliminated wet tailings disposal by constructing a dry tailings disposal facility and back-filling tunnels and shafts of the mine.
- avoided major stream diversions.
- eliminated a mixing zone in Lynn Canal, a fjord.

"We changed the treatment process in hopes of changing attitudes," notes Richins. Mertz acknowledged this change in attitude: "Throughout the last two years, we've developed a good deal of comfort with Coeur's straightforwardness and willingness to deal with the public as an equal partner." Even Juneau's most vocal and ardent mine critic found her attitudes and feelings altered somewhat by Coeur's direct and willing approach as she told Richins at the conclusion of the negotiations, "I'll never give you my support, but I'll agree not to come after you."

While there has been no direct litigation against the Kensington Mine, there still is no signed Kensington Agreement by the company or by the largest environmental group, SEACC, and two other environmental groups. Although these resisting groups certainly recognized progress, Mertz conceded that some groups apparently couldn't feel comfortable with the notion of ever signing onto a major mining project regardless of the details. With only half the groups agreeing and with the low price of gold forcing the engineers to go back to the drawing boards, Coeur Alaska opted not to sign the agreement either.

The real answer to the question, "Is the negotiation process worth it?" comes not from who signed and who didn't but from contrasting Coeur Alaska's tentative results with that of the other mine project—Echo Bay. As the permitting process got underway for Echo Bay, the project was quickly enveloped in controversies over water quality and tailings disposal in the Sheep Creek recreation area. With controversy rising, Echo Bay attempted to screen as much of the exploration process from the public view as possible. This tactic did not build trust. Instead it prompted legal challenges that delayed permits for exploration. It also prompted opponents to investigate and monitor the exploratory activities with more diligence. Before long, Echo Bay officials were in the position of making statements that critics were able to show as false and misleading. For example, Echo Bay claimed that their ongoing exploration activities made no illegal discharges into Gold Creek, a pubic water supply. Their critics countered with evidence showing otherwise. Once the criticism hit the local papers, government monitoring of mine discharges increased, ultimately resulting in EPA confirming illegal discharges of pollution into Gold Creek.

A few months later, Echo Bay announced the closing of their operations due to the low price of gold. The community of Juneau was not at all surprised when an FBI investigation later confirmed Echo Bay falsified records and covered up illegal discharges into Gold Creek.

Despite their controversial approach to mine permitting, Echo Bay still represented jobs and economic diversification. As such, they managed to hold on to support in some influential political corners. "Regardless of how 'in your face' they might have been, Echo Bay knew that the likelihood of getting city permits was still promising, but they might not have received permits as soon, and those permits would have had more baggage—stiff conditions," speculated Murray Walsh, who then headed the municipality's Community Development Department.[73] Mr. Walsh also points out that while the price of gold, down 25 percent, certainly affected the outcome of the Echo Bay project, their mine had a distinct advantage over the Kensington Mine because it had 5 million ounces of proven reserves, five times what most mines have, going into permitting. "Given all the controversy with Echo Bay, once the price of gold dropped, it was easier to say 'we quit.' Coeur Alaska is still in the running," concluded Walsh.

Richens from Coeur Alaska contrasted the results in this way:

> "The most positive aspect of the Agreement was the dialogue that brought the groups and the company to the table, where we considered their input on the front end of the project. Their ideas were incorporated into the environmental design of the project. Another benefit is the intangible of investment confidence. The investment community watches the front end of projects much more closely than they used to. They know that major lawsuits affect stock prices. And while we don't have a commitment to no lawsuits, we are not being sued and we have a record to point to that says we are being environmentally responsible. Echo Bay mine is closed, and if the project were still alive they would have no such record."

But back to answering an earlier question, "Is the negotiations process worth it?" Compared to lawsuits, do negotiations do a better job of reaching an agreement? While the answer for Couer Alaska was "yes," the real answer for many environmental disputes is "it depends." It depends on a whole suite of factors, like whether or not the dispute is ripe for settlement. But setting these factors aside and just looking at the end result of reaching an agreement, I wonder, is there any appreciable difference between environmental disputes in litigation and those not? Shedding some light on this question is the legal research done by Gail Bingham, author of

Resolving Environmental Disputes.[74] Ms. Bingham selected 99 site-specific environmental disputes and sorted these cases by the end result of whether or not agreement was successfully reached by opposing parties. She then examined the status of litigation. She found that of the 49 site-specific cases not in litigation, 88 percent reached agreement. For the cases where a lawsuit was filed, parties were able to reach agreement 78 percent of the time. So litigation appears to have been a hindrance in ten percent of the environmental cases she evaluated. Though this difference is slight, it still makes negotiations an attractive alternative, particularly if the "it depends" factors exist for the particular dispute.

The first thing mediation professionals will tell you is that citizen collaboration is not a magic potion for resolving every environmental conflict. According to Gerald Mueller of Missoula, Montana, who has been a professional mediator since 1988, "Collaboration doesn't work for groups at the point of hanging someone in effigy or actually committing violence."[75] Nor does collaboration work for people trying to determine rights or obtain justice for past wrongs.

In an article, entitled "Some Not-so-easy Steps to Successful Collaboration," Mr. Mueller notes these ingredients must exist for successful collaboration:

- A feeling that something must change
- A focus on the future
- The presence of relevant people—all stakeholders
- Strong civic leadership
- Moral—but not legal—authority

"Are people ready to do something different?" asks Mueller. "If they want to perpetuate the status quo, they'll continue to do that." Mr. Mueller also stresses the importance of stakeholder involvement. "Generally these groups come up with some recommendations they take to a body, an administrator or legislature. To the extent that they've had all the stakeholders present, everyone I've been involved with has been accepted." Other mediators caution that it's important to limit the decision-making ability to those parties that have a direct stake in the outcome and to exclude those with fundamental irresolvable differences. Similarly, it's helpful to exclude those participants that are in the dispute more for the show than for substantive resolution. In enlarging the circle of affected users one must be wary about including participants without a direct stake in the outcome of the natural resource dispute. Those without a direct stake, yet given standing in the decision-making process, are likely to introduce values and issues that are tangential, outside the resource issue at hand. And many of us are aware that extraneous issues make it more difficult to find on-target, consensus-driven solutions. Enlarging the web effect of affected industries and jobs must be tempered by the need to keep the decision-making process manageable and on track. It is often better to have a small well-placed web of resource users, than a cacophony of outraged, superfluous interest groups.

In terms of costs, goodwill and just mere "getting on with business," there is considerable value in community collaboration efforts and many rural communities are recognizing this. Rural news writer Lisa Jones notes:

> "Coalitions of environmentalists, ranchers, county commissioners, government officials, loggers, skiers, and jeepers are popping up as often as wood ticks across the Western landscape. Nobody is keeping an accurate count of this up swell. West side, there are about 70 coalitions organized around watersheds. Five Western universities teach natural-resource conflict resolution, and a periodical devoted to collaboration will begin publication in Montana this summer. Resolving conflict is a growth business."[76]

The Western Governors Association is even advancing collaboration among stakeholders. "Collaboration, Not Polarization" is one of eight principles endorsed by the Western Governors

Association as they recognize that to "succeed at environmental management people need to be empowered to do the right thing." In this regard, the Governors understand that collaborative processes break down barriers and lead to solutions for an array of environmental problems facing the residents of their states. These Governors emphasize collaboration as a direct attempt to minimize using the judicial process as a way to make decisions on environmental issues.[77]

Part of the upswell in forming conservation partnerships and community resolution groups is a result of losing faith in the federal government and/or the courts to solve complex, ever-changing, resource management problems. Missoula Mayor and author Daniel Kemmis captures this sentiment best:

> "I do not believe the federal government has the capacity to manage the West. I do not believe, either, that any solution coming from one end of the political spectrum or the other is going to have the capacity to do what this landscape requires.... The bottom line would be to say that we want and we need control over our own land. We do not expect to be given that control until we get our own act together."[78]

For many rural environmentalists and business leaders, getting one's act together means forming a group capable of representing the array of interests caught up in the particular resource issue. Getting one's act together also means tapping into:

Eco-nomic Principle No. 5
Maximize the Buy-In to Minimize the Conflict

The more directly affected interests place their fingerprints on a proposed project or action, the less likely those interests will seek the lawsuit route. The more stakeholders buy in on either a procedural or substantive level, the more likely things can move forward out of court. If the right ingredients (see page 69) are present, seek formal collaboration of interests to resolve environmental or resource-use conflicts. Community-based collaboration is a growing alternative to lawsuits as more people learn that courts are not in the dispute-resolution business; they are about making the wrong side pay up. Time not spent litigating and appealing is time being proactive together to discover common interests and solutions. Solutions agreed to by all stakeholders significantly enhance acceptance and implementation by legislative and/or administrative bodies. The more the buy in, the more likely the solution will stick.

Former EPA Administrator William R. Ruckleshaus echoes this principle when talking about collaboration among watershed users. He states, "We all talk about sustainable development, sustainable fisheries, what you get out of these [collaboration] processes if you are successful is a sustainable solution because the people who have bought into it are the very people most dramatically affected, and therefore if they buy into it then it will stick."[79]

Still doubtful, Don Snow, Executive Director of Northern Lights Institute, a group involved in mediation for 10 years, offers these words of encouragement:

> "You'll have much greater gain doing this [community collaboration] than as a bunch of road warriors who flash into the legislature and put laws onto agencies who have the power of the lion in *The Wizard of Oz*. I say to environmentalists this isn't to be feared; this is your [policy] accomplishment of the last 30 years. It's actually a very logical outgrowth. We've done a lot on paper. Now it's time to get it on the ground."[80]

Don Snow hits the hammer on the head. The opportunity to seek collaborative solutions to resource conflict is the policy accomplishment of earlier environmentalist. Don't deny this accomplishment, use it. Seek mediation or conflict resolution services as an alternative to traditional institutional decision-making because:

- Often, not all affected stakeholders have adequate or equal access to administrative or legislative decision-making. This exposes the decision to future challenges by a disenfranchised group or individual.
- Courts are not primarily in the dispute resolution business; they are really in the business of making the wrong side pay up. Enforcement, not conflict resolution, is what courts largely accomplish.
- Judges lack expertise on technical environmental issues. Similarly, legislators may understand little about site-specific environmental disputes. Administrative personnel may have the environmental knowledge but they are often perceived as an involved party in the dispute.
- Attitudes toward the role of government, the courts and private institutions are shifting. Participatory decision-making is more the expected rule than the exception.
- The call for "sustainability" or "collaborative stewardship" in decision-making requires more integration of economic, social and environmental considerations.
- Costly delays are common when seeking judicial or legislative resolution.
- More traditional approaches to resolving resource allocation or management disputes are limited by procedural shortcomings, i.e. the 5-minute "state your name for the record" drill.

CHAPTER 6

Beyond the Forest Wars:

Respect and Ecosystem Management

Forest wars have ignited throughout the West. Some fires are easily contained in the arena of public appeals, but some forest wars crown-up into all-out community conflict, pitting neighbor against neighbor. As a resident of the Tongass National Forest, the nation's largest national forest, I've seen how the flames of controversy fuel death threats and scar the community fabric. As an armchair observer of forest conflict elsewhere, I am awed at the resiliency and adaptability of forest-dependent communities. Just like after a wildfire, new growth and renewed productivity spring up after the flames of controversy pass through the city halls, the legislatures and the courts.

This chapter briefly explores two forest wars: a local one in Northern California on the verge of setting national precedent, and the spotted owl war. These two forest wars are in their final stages and would be generally considered contained, but hot spots still show up. As we dig into the ashes of a forest fire, we often find healthy roots. Similarly, we find the roots of many timber towns capable of and indeed sprouting new growth. Because of the nationally charged rhetoric surrounding the spotted owl controversy, it is enlightening and sobering to look back at what occurred in these timber-dependent communities. Who won the war? Did these flare-ups have to occur at all? A good place to start answering these questions is in northwest California in the town of Quincy, population 5,000.

The Quincy Library Group

(This account is based on the thorough reporting done by Ed Marston, publisher of *High Country News*, September 29, 1997)

To the casual observer, there is nothing to show that Quincy's approach to conflict resolution represents the most serious challenge to the environmental movement in decades. To the inside political observer, it comes as a total surprise that a plan authored by the Quincy Library Group would be the basis for arch-enemies, Rep. Don Young of Alaska and Rep. George Miller of California, to agree on national legislation and thereby pave the way for an unprecedented vote of 429 to 1 on a natural resource issue.[81]

It started in 1992. Then county supervisor Bill Coates, fearful for his community's well-being, decided there had to be an alternative to the repetitive lobbying trips to D.C. asking for more timber, followed by cycles of appeals and injunctions by a local environmental attorney. The lack of timber was now being felt in the schools, in the town's utilities and in the everyday life of Quincy. Long-standing residents were starting to leave. Bill Coates saw his community disintegrating. He reached out to Michael Jackson, the town's environmental lawyer. As Jackson tells it, "Mr. Coates said, 'All right we're through. We've got to do something new. Will you meet with the mill owners?'"[82] Despite the bullet holes in his office windows and a death threat, Michael Jackson agreed to meet with Coates and Tom Nelson, chief forester at Sierra Pacific Industries, the town's only sawmill. To Jackson, healing the community's wound was attractive, so he signed on for what he thought would be a short ride.

They initially met in the back room of Jackson's office. "They [the meetings] were supposed to be secret," Jackson says, "but it was clear to everyone that something was going on, and [secrecy] wasn't acceptable to anyone. So the next meeting was in the Quincy Library where anyone could listen in."[83] The Quincy Library Group had been born.

By looking carefully at their local forests, they discovered that if they set aside the local wilderness areas, the national parks and the biologically sensitive areas as proposed by environmentalist in 1986, they still had large amounts of forest open for sustainable timber harvest. Mike Yost, a local forestry professor, recalls the computer and map work that led to the plan: "We basically protected all the land we could—streams, roadless area, old growth—and then told the computer to thin the remaining (roaded) forest heavily. We were trying to show there was volume out there."[84]

They discovered that there was a perceived resource scarcity on one hand, and a perceived resource abundance on the other. Industry learned that volume existed outside the protected areas, and the environmental community learned that for the last ten years the Forest Service had kept Quincy at war by publicly suggesting that the protected areas represented huge amounts of timber.

The Quincy Library Group had learned the same thing that professional environmental mediators have learned over the years. They learned that more often than not, resource scarcity is a *perceived* and not an *actual* scarcity, or at least the scarcity is not as severe as perceived. Often, perceived resource scarcity accentuates destructive environmental conflicts. In his book, *Resolving Environmental Conflict*, mediator Chris Maser notes, "I am convinced that destructive environmental conflicts arise from a deep, albeit unconscious, sense of potential loss—a chronic or acute fear of the future based on a socialized disaster mentality."[85] Oregon State Professor William Krueger concurs: "The prevailing attitude in American society today is that we are short of resources (time, money, water, wildlife, etc.) and so must struggle to allocate them among competing demands. This attitude may be the basis of unnecessary conflict in natural resource management."[86]

Unnecessary or not, the conflict in Quincy was real. Wanting to evaluate actual timber availability, the Quincy Library Group ran the numbers again. Based on revised volume analysis, they allocated 1.6 million acres to timber harvest—the same lands in need of thinning and clearing to reduce fire risk—and 150,000 acres off-limits to logging. The environmentalists also got expanded protection of riparian zones and an end to 40-acre clear cuts in favor of smaller forest openings. Coates, Jackson, and Nelson dubbed the plan, the "Community Stability Proposal." In the end, neither side left the negotiating table, feeling they had compromised. "The only thing I gave up was my prejudices," notes Jackson.[87]

Proposal in place, the three conspirators called a town meeting to explain the plan. They put the proposal to a straw vote. Two hundred forty-five residents wanted to move forward with the plan, five said no. Two of those voting no were environmental die-hard friends of Jackson, and three were industry die-hard friends of Nelson. This was a 98-percent vote of confidence. Jackson calls the people on the fringe "wing nuts" and says they play the role of keeping the center together.[88]

An agreement in principle is one thing. Translating it onto the ground is quite another. So the Quincy Library Group brought in well-known experts in the fields of ecosystem management, silviculture and fire suppression to lay out how the principles were to be implemented on the ground. The Community Stability Plan was altered to incorporate the suggestions of government scientists. With this reality check and an Implementation Plan under their arms, the Quincy Library Group went to the Forest Service to seek their cooperation. They asked that forest plans be amended to account for their complete, comprehensive Community Stability Proposal. However, failing to recognize this "gift of local consensus" backed by their science no less, the Forest Service opted to sit on the plan. They sat on the plan for years, even when told otherwise by then Forest Service Chief Jack Ward Thomas. In a 1994 meeting with the Quincy Library Group, Chief Thomas instructed his forest supervisors to "work with them." Despite that message, no course was ever set on the ground. Kent Cannaughton, a local forest supervisor, says Jackson did not understand the agency. "If he is looking for a prime mover, the Forest Service is akin to an organism and no one individual can move it. Everyone has to want to move in the same direction."[89]

Undaunted by the inertia of the federal organism, the Quincy Library Group went next to Congress. Rep. Wally Herger introduced a bill ordering the Forest Service to do the group's bidding, the Forest Service showed its true colors. They opposed the "Community Stability Plan" because national forest plans shouldn't be decided by local consensus. National environmental groups also saw this as a threat to their sphere of influence and control. It didn't take long before 140 national and regional groups opposed the bill. Jim Lyons, Undersecretary of Agriculture, explained the opposition this way:

> "This pilot [project] represents a threat to the national environmental leadership and its capacity to dictate the terms of the agreement to the local scale, and the national groups are not quite sure how to handle it. I think they are very concerned about Quincy Library Groups popping up all over the place. It is a legitimate concern. We don't want to manage national forest based on local consensus."[90]

With this prevailing anti-local sentiment, it was only a matter of time before the Quincy Library Group bill was hijacked—by the national timber industry. Rep. Don Young of Alaska, on behalf of the timber industry, agreed to amend the bill to exempt 2.5 million acres from federal environmental law. Rep. George Miller, a strong supporter of the national environmental groups, countered. And as most political observers know, for every resource action by Rep. Young, there is an equal and opposite Miller reaction. Then it became Miller time. Only this time the opposite reaction was to amend the bill back to the Quincy Library Group's original version and support it despite the opposition by his traditional allies, the national groups. Enveloped in irony Rep. Miller, nonetheless, took his plan to Young. He agreed, and the bill requiring the Forest Service to stick to the Quincy Library Group plan with no exemptions passed the House 429 to 1.[91]

Senator Diane Feinstein from California hones in on the

fundamental question of local collaborative groups resolving national environmental issues. She states in a December 1997 letter:

> I sincerely believe that opposition from environmentalists on the national level is really philosophical in that people believe the Quincy Library Group bill is an exemption to federal law and they do not want it to succeed. The Quincy Library Group proposal is intended to reduce the risk of fire, restore forest health, and provide community stability with an adequate timber supply for local mills. My own view is that the law should allow the consensus achieved by the Quincy Library Group to have an opportunity to be tested. In five years, we will know whether this pilot project works, or not and whether local collaborative groups can in fact succeed in solving this kind of problem. That to me is the challenge.[92]

One must wonder about a system that makes it so difficult for a Quincy Library Group effort to succeed. This local group was created to replace contention with civility, to replace distrust with respect, to replace conflict with shared community vision. The trust and respect was so strong that when asked about the concern of loggers and ranchers end running the environmentalists, Jackson responded:

> Do I worry about being tricked? No. I know courtroom tricks I haven't even begun to use. I know national editorial writers. I have lots of abilities and I want them to be community abilities. And my friends in the timber industry have abilities that should be community abilities. We're much stronger together. We now share what we know.[93]

And now thanks to ironic Congressional action, Jackson reaps the benefits of putting community first, "These days, when people wave at me, they use all five fingers," he proclaims.[94] On a national conscience level, shouldn't we want the Jacksons, Coates and Nelsons of the rural West to succeed, particularly since research shows that the environment is primarily a local issue? If Americans worry most about quality of life in their own communities, what is wrong with stakeholder consensus groups that represent the prevailing national interests?

Take for example a coalition of farmers, ranchers, kayakers, sport fishers and agency officials working on salmon recovery in a tributary of the Snake River. The Henry's Fork of the Snake River is a blue ribbon, fly-fishing river in the heart of Idaho's potato country. Each local user of the river can pitch an argument of national importance, and each use bumps up against another use. Despite a rocky and acrimonious beginning, a coalition is now coming to terms on basic principles for a long-term solution. If this consensus organization, the Henry's Fork Watershed Council, continues to make progress in charting a recovery plan for salmon, shouldn't the National Forest constituency be pleased? Members of this Watershed Council recognize that "none of us is as smart as all of us."[95] Can the same be recognized by D.C. lobbyists whose funding is tied to membership drives touting singular accomplishments?

As noted in the previous chapter, these collaborative organizations are springing up all over the country. There are now hundreds of collaborative watershed groups all across the West. The Colorado River Basin has 70 groups alone.[96] These groups are engaged in everything from stream rehabilitation, from writing management plans to drafting strategies to reverse the effects of mining and ranching. In short these groups are attempting and succeeding to do what conventional public processes have failed to do—resolve resource disputes quickly and civilly. So why is it so hard for consensus solutions to succeed on a national level? Here are some responses to ponder:

- The stage of national politics promotes acting instead of sincerity.
- The national limelight is not necessarily conducive to respect replacing mistrust.
- The larger the number of people coming to the table, the more difficult it will be to find agreement.

- If you do reach agreement, the respect needed to keep it together is a lot harder to hold on to amidst the power plays and high agendas of national interest groups.

This is not to say it cannot occur at all on a national level. I once participated in a national consensus effort that was a success. At the suggestion of the House and Senate committee leadership in 1992, the conservation community and the fishing industry convened a series of meetings to draft consensus legislation for marine mammal protection. Led by the National Fisheries Institute and the Center for Marine Conservation, about 30 organizations, including the animal rights groups, came together to meet this Congressional challenge. The motivation to come together at this national level was strong. Everyone disagreed with the approach drafted by the National Marine Fisheries Service, and all sides felt that a better, more reality-based alternative could be found. Eventually, the agreement became the basis for Congressional Reauthorization of the Marine Mammal Protection Act. Looking back at this experience, Suzanne Iudicello, Senior Program Counsel for the Center for Marine Conservation, says this consensus effort with involved stakeholders was the exception and not the rule for most national environmental organizations. What aided this national effort, was: a) fewer groups, only 30 and, b) a moderate environmental organization with a history of working with industry. The Center for Marine Conservation took the initiative while the larger and more prominent environmental organizations looked the other way.[97] Nonetheless, this example suggests that in some circumstances, national consensus efforts can work as well as local efforts; only the challenge bar is trickier to clear.

Bringing the resource conflict back to the local arena does not necessarily lower the challenge bar for finding solutions to resource conflicts; it just makes it easier to see the bar. Instead of debating the issues in the newspapers, people debate them face-to-face. The issues are more transparent and real. This, however, doesn't mean they are any less intense. Economist Thomas Michael Power reminds us why the challenge bar remains high for rural communities: "Economic insecurity makes people desperate; it breeds the fear and hostility that has come to infect the debate over environmental policy in many rural communities."[98]

Economic insecurity is a powerful force that ignites in the face of extremists, in the "winner-take-all" rhetoric. When Forestry Professor Tom Bonnicksen was asked, "Is there a solution to the Forest Wars?" He replied:

> "We have to stop the winner-take-all attitude before the forest wars will end. And we can use one word to end the forest wars and that word is *respect*. Respect for all the life around us, and respect for the right and welfare of our fellow human beings."[99]

Mr. Bonnicksen's words bring me to:

Eco-nomic Principle No. 6
Seek Local Solutions Based on Respect

If we accept the idea that humans are part of ecosystems, then meaningful participation by those affected by the long-term health of that ecosystem is an essential element in any approach to ecosystem management. This drives ecosystem management and planning down to the local or regional level. Accepting this premise of human integration into ecosystem management should allow upper levels of management, both corporate and governmental, to accept a lower, locally generated solution. Getting to solutions invariably means resolving conflict. Progress in resolving conflict occurs when there is basic respect for the right and welfare of fellow human beings. The more problem-solving individuals see each other as neighbors needing to share the same ecosystem, the easier it is to let respect enter into the dispute and eventually become the glue that holds any agreement together. If all politics are local, why can't national political problems be solved locally? Go where the odds for respect prevailing are best; go where folks can appreciate that none of us are as smart as all of us; go local when given the chance.

The Quincy Library Group is an excellent example of respect prevailing. Both sides had chances to end-run the agreement when the administration and Congress changed party affiliations. When the Clinton administration arrived, many environmentalists thought the sky was the limit, but instead of working the system for more, Jackson and the local environmentalists stuck with the deal. When the Republicans took control of Congress, Jackson put the question to the timber industry, "Do we still have a deal? Are you going to honor your agreement, or are you going to back out?" Nelson, on behalf of the timber industry, responded, "No, a deal's a deal."[100]

Another good reason to go local is that in many areas, quality of life is as much defined by the natural environment as the human environment. Even in Alaska, a state dominated by extractive industries, university studies indicate that the most important contributions to quality in life are those elements associated with the natural environment: clean air and water, beauty of surrounding areas, and open, undeveloped areas.[101]

Now let's look into the aftermath of a forest war that quickly moved beyond local resolution: the northern spotted owl controversy which first flamed into national view in the 1990s. President Clinton stepped in, convened a conference, listened and eventually came up with a Forest Plan in 1993, which neither side liked. No surprise there. But what of President Clinton's Spotted Owl Forest Plan? Did economic havoc ensue? Are there any lessons here?

The Northern Spotted Owl

The best account of post-spotted owl life in the Pacific Northwest is from Daniel Glickman, a frequent contributor to *Newsweek* and *National Wildlife*. In an article entitled "Having Owls and Jobs Too," Daniel Glick notes that in Oregon, where protection of the northern spotted owl was supposed to destroy jobs, the opposite is occurring.

In 1995, just a few short years after President Clinton's plan to set lower timber harvests, Oregon's employment level of 4.6 percent was below the national level of 5.5 percent and property values were rising by 10 percent a year. Despite a loss of 14,300 jobs in the timber industry since 1988 and dire times for some rural mill towns, the Oregon economy more than made up for that sector's job losses with new jobs elsewhere. Many new jobs came from high-tech industries lured by the quality of life provided by the forest and the communities. The wood products industry also developed more efficient manufacturing techniques and expanded product lines. In 1995, the state's timber production still led the country at around five billion board feet a year.

Timber companies with vast tracts of second-growth forest have seen a rise in timber prices—in large part from the reduced public-lands supply. "It's been a windfall," says Boise Cascade director of communications Bob Hayes. By way of thanks for this economic turnaround, argues Andy Kerr, of the Oregon Natural Resources Council, "timber companies should send environmentalists thank you notes and nice big checks."[102]

Author Daniel Glickman contends that both Hayes and Kerr miss a critical point. So do loggers who blame or credit [Judge] Dwyer's ruling for changing their lives. The dirty little secret of the owl wars is that *Stix occidentalis caurina* is no more responsible for the boom in the state's economy than it is for job losses in the northwest timber industry.

"There's this myth that these changes would not have occurred but for the owl-recovery plan," says University of Oregon economist

Ed Whitelaw. "That is simply wrong," sighs Phil Keisling, Oregon's Secretary of State. "People have loaded so much baggage on the shoulders of this 15-inch bird."[103]

Even before the court-ordered moratorium on large tracts of old-growth forest, some wood-products business had been heading for a fall for reasons as complex as a forest ecosystem. Following record cuts from peak harvest years on public and private lands in the 1940s and 1950s, the forest had not been replanted for decades, leaving second-growth stocks far short of the 70 to 100 years needed for sustainable-yield cycles. Automation of lumber mills and logging also cut jobs. By the early 1990s, mill wages had declined and wood-products jobs had been more difficult to find for more than a decade.

The bottom line in Oregon's timber-dependent regions is that change was coming anyway. The spotted owl controversy just accentuated and politicized the change, a type of change often accompanied by pain and disruption. In looking back from the perspective of sociologists, one learns that some towns fared better than other towns. Some towns have a capacity to adapt, others don't. It's more than just a function of town size. The U.S. Forest Service research concludes that towns with the "capacity to adapt" are the towns with moderate diversity, core infrastructure, active leadership, and linkages to political and economic centers. A general resiliency was found in many small rural towns. In particular, many rural towns perceived by their residents as timber communities are fairly resilient and healthy, especially compared with small ranching and farming communities. These timber towns are already changing as a result of their amenities, diversifying economies, and shifting populations.[104]

Change and resiliency is the actual and desired image of many rural timber towns. In making this generalization, I do not intend to denigrate the pain and disruption caused by major economic changes in communities. Moving from the real forest to the silicon forest is not easy. For some it means retraining instead of retiring. It means letting go of your community's dominant identity. It means altering how you define yourself in generational terms. It means changing that collective understanding of what drives the local economy. It means addressing a town's economic insecurity head-on. But underneath is a resiliency that as economist Michael Powers notes converts concern for the environment into an asset:

> Rather than being an economic milestone around [rural] communities' necks, environmental quality has turned out to be the source of considerable economic growth. As a result, the choice extractive, resource-dependent communities face, as well as their likely futures, are nowhere as grim as portrayed by anti-environmentalists.[105]

Just like trucks in the rearview mirrors on our cars, past economic dependencies can loom larger than they appear. Fortunately, many communities with the capacity to adapt eventually see environmental quality as the rainbow in their rearview mirror. For some, economic calamity never looked so good.

The forest can be the same way. A natural calamity may look good 40-plus years later. Take for example a natural calamity—the 1936 hurricane of New England, a 100-mph-plus windstorm that devastated thousands of acres of hardwood forests throughout Connecticut and Massachusetts. Forty years later, these same devastated acres were home to a thriving diversified forest and served as my learning field while a student at the Yale School of Forestry and Environmental Studies. Change looked good, and I soon learned that ecologically speaking, forests of all kinds rely on disturbance. To quote my professor, David M. Smith:

> "The formative processes in the development of forest stands are disturbances that kill trees and make way for the new ones. The characteristics of all stands are determined by the kind, frequency, and magnitude of disturbances that have affected the sites in the past. Climax communities are, in this sense, results of long series of small light disturbances while pioneer stages are the product of catastrophe."[106]

As a forester, the objective then becomes developing a forest management plan where timber removals of climax species mimic the long series of small light disturbances. The fires of Yellowstone National Park in 1988 are a prime example of what happens when management aims to protect the forest from disturbances. One-half of this immense park was burned; most of it subjected to high-severity fire. Looking back, park ecologists concluded, "The fires were a direct result of protecting the forest." Lack of change/disturbance in the forest structure led to extreme fire consequences.

This attention to natural change in the context of fire harkens back to the Quincy Library Group. As you may remember, the Quincy Library Group hopes to avoid devastation by integrating harvest with computer simulations of high-severity fire risk. In their plan, timber harvest is more than removing merchantable wood from the forest, it is a proven way to reduce fuel buildup and provide fuel breaks in the likely event of a fire.

Ecosystem management applies the same principle of mimic disturbance and minimizing risk, only on a larger and more complex scale. Ecologist Dan Botkin, author of *Discordant Harmonies: A New Ecology for the Twenty-First Century,* says, "The message of modern ecology for environmentalists is action: If you do nothing, you will get something you do not expect."[107] Action is needed because change is a given. In tribute to the post-fire resilient roots of forests and communities, I offer:

Eco-nomic Principal No. 7
Change Is a Given

Understanding patterns of ecological change is part of promoting better environmental practices. Understanding the patterns of economic change is part of providing community stability. We can find solutions in mimicking or complementing the direction of change within the forests, the grasslands, and the oceans. Change is the dynamic constant in both ecological and economic systems. Therefore, fusing systems where possible and making changes beneficial to both man and nature is desirable and sometimes an achievable end. As the field of ecology branches out and grows into our everyday life, the real challenge here becomes one of trust to do right by man and nature; to practice ecosystem management and model sustainable development, knowing that we work and live in dynamic systems.

This begs the question: Is ecosystem management at all predictable? The ways in which ecosystems change is now partially predictable, thanks to a whole range of new technology from satellite imagery to radio tracking whales. Nonetheless, we cannot hold ecosystems constant or regulate them precisely. At best we can only guide. And at best we guide with the precautionary principle in mind. The precautionary principle means taking a conservative approach in the absence of good, reliable data.

In guiding these changes, we must keep in mind the image of a prescribed forest fire which is a fire purposely set to consume fuel buildup so that a following wildfire will be less damaging. Many times the desired effect of clearing and consuming dangerous levels of fuel buildup is achieved, but things can always go astray during the execution of a controlled burn. The wind can suddenly switch. The fire could head in an unintended direction.

Like the prescribed fire, guiding change is achievable, but can't be completely relied upon. We must always expect unforeseen change when dealing with the forces of nature. Often, just like in a wind-charged fire, the ecosystem is apt to look good 20 to 30 years later. Then by 100-plus years, a mature forest may hide the scars of ecosystem change.

So we either do nothing or still get change; or we trust our growing knowledge of how to influence and mimic ecological change for sustainability. Fortunately for us all, the field of ecosystem management is a growing, expanding field of knowledge.

Gaylord Nelson, Counselor to the Wilderness Society, sees this growth as a "scientific renaissance in land management":

> "Basic principles of ecosystem management—everything is connected to everything else, save all the parts, think like a mountain—had been with the modern conservation movement from its beginning, but the specifics of ecosystem management were elusive. Spurred by a growing recognition that many difficult environmental problems are really ecosystem problems, ecological principles began to work (again) into public land management policy and practice. Parallel to this scientific renaissance in land management was a great deal of administrative attention to finding new ways of resolving resource conflicts before they turn into train wrecks."[108]

The state-of-the-art report on ecosystem management has recently been published—*Ecosystem Management in the United States—An Assessment of Current Experiences.*[109] The University of Michigan collaborated with the Wilderness Society to catalog ecosystem management activities and to analyze the experiences of the people involved. Systematic interviews and surveys from an array of participants in 105 projects across the United States revealed some reassuring and interesting results.

When asked to state the goals of these ecosystem projects, the five most common goals cited were:

- to protect or preserve the ecosystem (most common)
- to restore the ecosystem
- to obtain stakeholder support
- to maintain or improve the local and regional economy
- to provide guidelines for ecosystem management

It is interesting to note that maintaining or improving the economy is in the mix of ecosystem management goals. This goal was especially important in the northwest and southwest where many economies are resource based.

To achieve the above-stated goals, project managers had to design numerous strategies applicable to the local area. The six most commonly reported strategies were:

- research
- stakeholder involvement
- ecosystem restoration
- promotion of compatible land uses
- education and outreach
- setting land aside

Note that several of these goals and strategies are very people oriented. In these projects, ecosystem management clearly entails human choices. "Many respondents noted that it was imperative for the success of ecosystem management projects that all stakeholders be involved in development and implementation of project activities."

The five outcomes of these ecosystem management projects tend to be procedural in nature such as development of decision-making structures and changes in approach to land management. While these process achievements establish relationships and management approaches, they are still likely to lead to on-the-ground ecological results. As one project manager concluded, "It appears that small successes at improving the process of management will motivate larger successes that can be measured in ecological terms in the future."

This brings us back to Eco-nomic Principle No. 7 . . . with change as a given, procedural success today can equate to substantive ecological success tomorrow. For example, one-third of the surveyed projects reported actual ecosystem restoration results while half of the projects reported ongoing ecosystem restoration.

These restoration results, while tentative in nature, show that we can exert a caring intellect toward ecosystem management.

Rachel Carson recognizes the inevitability of making choices and thereby trusting caring intellect:

> The earth's vegetation is part of a web of life in which there are intimate and essential relations. Sometimes we have no choice but to disturb these relationships, but we should do so thoughtfully, with full awareness that what we do may have consequences remote in time and place.

One of the places we as a society have no choice but to disturb the forest is in meeting our demand for wood, one of nature's wonder materials. In the bigger picture of environmental impacts, systematic, selective removal of timber may be one of our better choices. An analysis done for an international forestry conference in 1992 estimated that the energy and atmospheric costs of replacing one billion board feet of timber now used for U.S. home construction with products derived from steel, aluminum, concrete and brick might consume as much as 700 million more gallons of oil and produce an extra 7.5 tons of carbon dioxide.[110] Given these environmental costs, staying with renewable, recyclable and biodegradable wood is a better option.

Presently, U.S. timber harvests are not even keeping up with annual timber growth. For example, in 1996 the annual growth in our nation's forests exceeds annual harvest and mortality by 33 percent. Much of this growth is from the Eastern forests, from land once cleared in vast swathes. In the early nineteenth century, a cleric traveling from Boston to New York wrote in his record, "The forests are not only cut down, but there appears little reason to hope they will ever grow again."

Almost two hundred years later, despite great increases in population, 90 percent of New Hampshire is covered by forest. Vermont was 35 percent woods in 1850 and is 80 percent today. By the 1960s and 1970s, the pattern of forest and field was similar to that before 1800.[111] As our forests come full circle, so does the forest yield.

We can harvest a full rotation of timber production with forestry that works with the environment, not against it. Today, many progressive foresters ask not what to take but what to leave for wildlife, fish, recreation and diversity, and then figure out how to maximize the value of what remains for possible harvest.

Forestry is making a paradigm shift in thinking. Some specialists call it "new forestry," others say "environmental forestry," and some see it as part of ecosystem management. Others see it as just a new name for interdisciplinary silviculture. Whatever the name for this ecological thinking, the bottom line is that in the big picture of resource management, we can manage forests for the ecological removal of timber.

Moving beyond the forest, the bottom-line question is, "Are we willing to trust our knowledge to practice sustainable development?" While we're relatively young in inoculating sustainable development into regional and national economies, I can't help but be awed by the rate of innovative, meaningful technology. In an effort to answer this fundamental question of knowledge trust, try to list which of today's important technologies could have been imagined fifty years ago . . . fiber optics, compact discs, satellite imagery, electromagnetic body scanners, lasers, radars, cell phones, solar cells and of course the computer that pervades every facet of our modern life. Who would have thought that we would be practicing ecosystem management with the tools of satellite tracking, GPS mapping, computer simulation and carbon dating? Who imagined trapping toxic gases and converting them back into liquid form for reuse in the production process? Who could have imagined recycling toxic gases when the environmental movement first flourished in the aftermath of Love Canal? We are even figuring out how to produce hydrogen fuel cells for electricity with the only by-product being water.[112] If we can produce clean energy and recycle toxic gases, we are capable of growing sustainable economies. I believe that between technological advances and the global marketplace, the practice of sustainable development will mature in ways not yet conceived. We can trust our growing ecological intellect and respect our neighbor. If we can grasp hydrogen fuel cells, we are indeed capable of dreaming and actualizing big, and to do so is part of being a better angel of our human nature.

CHAPTER 7

Ecology Is Economy Is Ecology

Besides the *eco* similarity in sound, there is a similarity in design between nature's household—ecology, and humanity's household—economics. Both households run on efficiency and diversity. Waste in either system is often consumed. Both systems, from El Nino to the Asian economic flu, bring us daily reminders that we live in a global world. These systems that dominate our lives are intertwined in many, many ways—well beyond just eating Ben and Jerry's Rainforest Crunch ice cream. Economist Paul Hawkens concurs, "When you look at this issue of the environment and business, you're looking at the two great systems that dominate our lives: the natural system and the commercial-industrial systems."[113]

This chapter moves beyond the spotted owl situation in challenging the long-held assumption that environmental protection equates to job loss and replaces this myth with the theory that environmental responsibility is good for business. In the end, I hope to show that ecology is economy and that we need to act locally and globally to fuse these systems.

At the local level, whenever a manufacturing plant closes its door, environmental regulation is often indicted as the culprit of the demise. Rather than just accept this as a regrettable reality, the Institute for Southern Studies and the Economic Policy Institute both convened studies to challenge this commonly held association. The Institute of Southern Studies first published in 1994 the *Green is Gold* report.[114]

The approach taken by the Institute of Southern Studies was simple in design. For each state, researchers examined a range of statewide economic and environmental indicators and searched for correlations between the indices. Did the states with poor economic performance, as measured by 20 standardized indices (e.g., annual pay, unemployment, business start-ups) also have poor environmental performances as indicated by 20 environmental indices (e.g., toxic emissions, energy consumption, solid waste)? Was there any correlation? Did the states with strong economies have good environmental quality? States were ranked on each indicator, and the sum of ranks produced a state's final score.

Comparing the two lists of scores, they found:

- Nine states rank among the top twelve states on both the economic and environmental scales. They are Hawaii, Vermont, New Hampshire, Minnesota, Wisconsin, Colorado, Oregon, Massachusetts and Maryland.
- Conversely, twelve states are among the worst fourteen on both lists. Louisiana ranked last on both lists. The states most dependent on mining and oil wells generally faired the poorest on both lists.
- States that ranked best on the bellwether indicator of low infant mortality generally scored high on both lists.

Stephen M. Meyer of the Massachusetts Institute of Technology found that his twenty years of economic-performance analysis support these findings reported in the *Gold and Green*. Says Meyer: "States with stronger environmental standards tended to have the higher growth in their gross state products, total employment, construction employment, and labor productivity than states that ranked lower environmentally."[115]

At the conclusion of his indices analysis, senior author of *Gold and Green* Bob Hall writes: "At the policy level, the choice is really not jobs vs. the environment. The states that do more to protect their natural resources also wind up with the strongest economies and best jobs for their citizens."[116]

Economics Professor E.B. Goodstein of the Economic Policy Institute took a different analytical approach to this jobs versus environment question. He relied on regional economic studies and Department of Labor surveys of plant shutdowns. With an eye to the future, Mr. Goodstein reviewed two decades of analysis on the relationship between employment and environmental protection. He reported his findings in a report entitled "Jobs and the Environment: The Myth of a National Trade-Off." Some of his most intriguing results are as follows:

1) In a survey covering 57 percent of the manufacturing work force, the Department of Labor found four layoff events attributable to environmental or safety problems. Extrapolating this data to include all manufacturing jobs—1,300 lost positions per year, on average, could be partially attributed to environmental regulation. By comparison, forty times more layoffs resulted from ownership changes than from environmental protections measures.
2) Environmental protection expenses alone are simply not large enough to cripple an otherwise healthy plant. However, stringent pollution regulations might serve as the straw that breaks the camels back by making production unprofitable at certain localities. Yet, fears of such effects from pollution-control efforts are liable to be greatly overblown since industry officials can gain politically by blaming plant shutdowns due to normal business causes on environmental regulations.
3) On balance, the available studies [from 1978-1993] show that environmental protection spending—either because of its high domestic hire component or labor intensity—has probably led to a net increase in the number of jobs in the U.S. economy.
4) Highly polluting industries are relocating to poor countries. The reason, however, is primarily low wages, not environmental regulation. For those industries that remain in the U.S., pollution-control efforts can spur productivity by forcing firms

to adopt new and cheaper production techniques. For example, rather than installing end-of-the-pipe equipment to treat their emissions, some firms have developed new production methods to aggressively reduce waste, cutting both costs and pollution simultaneously.

5) Local tradeoffs can be significant in extractive industries. Even here, however, more conventional sources of job loss typically dominate. Moreover, job loss will typically be balanced by job growth in industries providing substitute products for the locked-up resource as well as those industries dependent on an undamaged environment.[117]

Mr. Goodstein's findings clearly weaken the jobs-versus-environment contention. Mr. Goodstein states, "At the national level, claims of a tradeoff between jobs and the environment are completely without substance."

While it is always enlightening to read these results from macro-level economic studies, i.e. national and state level, I like to find validation in the field or at the local level. For instance, can we manage forests for biodiversity and still create more jobs? University of Washington Forestry Professor Bruce Lippke says yes. With the aid of an economic model, Lippke compared employment under fifty-year rotations with employment under longer rotations and regular tree thinning operations, i.e., managing for yield and financial return compared to managing for yield and biodiversity. He found that managing for biodiversity doubled the economic activity of the short rotations common under industrialized forestry. Not only did primary processing jobs increase under the biodiversity management regime, but so did the secondary manufacturing jobs. This increase of secondary jobs was a direct result of the higher-quality wood produced by three tree thinnings. Lippke and Fretwell's analysis shows that in forestry there doesn't necessarily have to be a tradeoff between managing for economic returns or biodiversity.[118]

If plant shutdowns rarely occur because of environmental regulations; if environmental protection spending results in a net increase of national jobs; if managing forests for sustained yield and biodiversity creates more economic activity, then we could consider replacing:

environmental protection = job loss
with
good environment = good economics

Let's start with the notion that green businesses such as Ben and Jerry's Ice Cream and the 3M companies of America are generally good for the environment; that going green (e.g. recycling, polluting less, using less energy) is good for nature. If one can accept that going "green" as a business is better for the environment, then the key questions are: 1) Is it good for the company's bottom line? and, 2) Is it more than just good public relations? Let us consider accounts from some prominent American companies.

3M company spokesperson Rick Renner notes that by "getting ahead of regulations" the company has cut its waste output by about one-third and air pollution by seventy percent since 1990. Over the last twenty years, pollution-prevention measures have saved 3M more than $710 million.[119] This brought home the message that it is cheaper to deal with pollution before it goes into the pipe rather than when it comes out of the pipe. This 94-year-old manufacturing company demonstrates conclusively that the bottom line of green is black.

Then there is the growing war on waste. At last, a war headline I was heartened to see:

New War on Waste

Leading the way in the battle against waste is Baxter International, a medical-products maker located in Deerfield, Illinois. According to their 2001 report, Baxter International is now reaping a whopping $53 million in savings from energy and water reductions, improved waste disposal methods and recycling for seven years.[120] Turns out this war on waste provided about 10 percent of the company's net income for 2001.

Seattle City Light now spends more than 4 percent of its annual revenues on promoting conservation.[121] Seattle City Light, like other progressive utilities, has discovered that convincing consumers to use less energy is more economical than building a new generating facility. Instead of trying to sell consumers on using more energy, many utilities now have a budget item for energy conservation. This is a complete reversal from past utility practices.

Economist, professor and author Michael Silverstein explains that corporate environmental actions are here to stay:

> "Every major sector of the U.S. economy, every manufacturing and marketing component, is today undergoing an environmental restructuring aimed at making it more efficient and less wasteful, less prone to clean-up liabilities in years to come, and better able to tap burgeoning consumer demand for greener products and services."[122]

Senior Policy Analyst (Department of Energy) Joseph Romm, author of *Lean and Clean Management,* sees the same trend:

> "The best companies no longer see pollution as an inevitable by-product of the way they do business. But rather, pollution is simply a measure of their inefficiency. Pollution is waste and the best companies now measure it, track it, and try to reduce it over time."[123]

The World Resources Institute, a Washington, D.C., think tank, compared the exporting prowess of U.S. companies that face strict environmental regulation with the U.S. industry as a whole. Using World Bank data, economist Robert Repetto discovered that U.S. companies were subject to the most stringent regulations and were more competitive than companies operating under less strict oversight.[124] Sun Oil Company, a company subject to stringent oversight, touts this message in their paid advertisements: "We run a business, and this is a business decision. We believe that the future belongs to those companies that see environmental protection as a valued condition for economic growth."

While making a difference to the bottom line is a strong motivator for many companies like Sun Oil to use less, to convert waste into by-products and to recycle, another equally important motivator for doing right by the environment is reputation. "Reputation is increasingly seen as something more than the record of earnings growth rates," says Robert Waterman Jr., co-author of *In Search of Excellence*. "In the knowledge economy a company's reputation and the generally held sense of identity takes on heightened value."[125]

In *Fortune* magazine's annual determination of America's most admired companies, environmental responsibility is one of eight rating categories. Rubbermaid topped the list in 1995. Rubbermaid's reputation for environmental responsibility played a significant role in their high rating. Today Rubbermaid is recognized as a leader in the recovery and reuse of low-density polyethylene stretch wrap and plastic pellets.[126]

A 1997 study of more than 300 S&P-500 companies by ICF/Kaiser, an investment firm, confirmed the validity of environmental responsibility as central to a company's market-vulnerable reputation. This study concluded that "adopting a more environmentally proactive posture has, in addition to any direct environmental and cost-reduction benefits, a significant and favorable impact on the firm's perceived riskiness to investors and, accordingly, its cost of equity capital and value in the marketplace."[127]

Environmental responsibility principles are now part of many companies' guidelines, either directly through management or indirectly through the Chamber of Commerce network. For example, the International Chamber of Commerce's Business

Charter for Sustainable Development commits their membership of 7,500 companies and business organizations to sixteen principles for environmental management.

Number 1 on their list is "to recognize environmental management as among the *highest* (emphasis added) corporate priorities and as a key determinant to sustainable development; to establish policies, programs and practices for conducting operations in an environmentally sound manner."[128] Judging by the attitude of some local Chambers of Commerce, you would never know this policy existed, let alone, was a priority.

Today, many companies have made the turn around from the "dirty dozen" to the "most admired." Hewlett Packard is one such company. In 1988, Hewlett Packard was cited by the Silicon Valley Toxic Coalition, a local environmental activist group, as one if its dirty dozen toxic polluters. Since then, Hewlett Packard has eliminated use of chlorofluorocarbons and several other ozone-depleting compounds two years ahead of the 1995 deadline. Over a four-year period (1990-94), Hewlett Packard reduced their releases of toxic chemicals into the environment by nearly 80 percent. Out of recognition for these changes, *Fortune* magazine named Hewlett Packard America's Most Admired Computer/Office Equipment Company.[129]

"We have been successful in introducing environmental quality as a value in the decision making of corporate America," notes Pamela Lippe, executive direction of Earth Day New York and head of the national Earth Day Network.[130] It is time for the environmental communities to reap the inoculation benefits of the last three decades of environmental legislation, regulation and public education. It is time to accept environmental responsibility as part of the corporate culture in America. Why not accept it if it works for the environment?

Personally, I'm jazzed to have the power of the marketplace in pursuing sustainable development. Dramatic progress in sustainable communities will not be made through legislation and regulation alone; and as symbolized by the fall of the Berlin Wall, the global marketplace is a powerful agent of change. I still remember watching the demonstrations throughout Eastern Europe leading right up to the toppling of the wall. I still remember the tingling sensation of "cold war over" rising in my consciousness as I watched the first section tumble under the freed feet of the East Berliners. What a joyful, redeeming moment of humanity, made possible by forces beyond government. While far less symbolic and important, I couldn't help but feel a similar degree of awe at the power of the global marketplace when viewing the first green, multimillion, 30-second spot on Superbowl Sunday. The commercial was not a Nike, Coca-Cola, or Budweiser commercial, rather it was a 3M commercial touting their environmental accomplishments rising above and beyond compliance. What I saw in this commercial was more than the warm, fuzzy, do-good feeling that the 3M company projected. I saw the same potential power that the marketplace exerted in gradually eroding the Berlin Wall being transferred to the arena of environmental responsibility. Connecting the marketplace into environmental reform on a global scale is the mission behind the Coalition for Environmentally Responsible Economies (CERES).[131]

The CERES coalition was formed in 1989. It brought fifteen major U.S. environmental groups together with an array of socially responsible investors and public pension funds representing more than *$150 billion* in invested capital. With that kind of money, over the past nine years CERES has emerged as a worldwide leader in pioneering an innovative, practical approach toward encouraging greater corporate responsibility on environmental issues. They start by getting Companies to sign onto these forward-thinking principles:

The CERES Principles

Protection of the Biosphere. We will reduce and make continual progress toward eliminating the release of any substance that may cause environmental damage to the air, water, or the earth or its inhabitants. We will safeguard all habitats affected by our operations and will protect open spaces and wilderness, while preserving biodiversity.

Sustainable Use of Natural Resources. We will make sustainable use of renewable natural resources, such as water, soils, and forests. We will conserve non-renewable natural resources through efficient use and careful planning.

Reduction and Disposal of Wastes. We will reduce and, where possible, eliminate waste through source reduction and recycling. All wastes will be handled and disposed of through sage and responsible methods.

Energy Conservation. We will conserve energy and improve the energy efficiency of our internal operations and of the goods and services we sell. We will make every effort to use environmentally safe and sustainable energy sources.

Risk Reduction. We will strive to minimize the environmental, health and safety risks to our employees and the communities in which we operate through safe technologies, facilities and operating procedures, and by being prepared for emergencies.

Safe Products and Services. We will reduce and, where possible, eliminate the use, manufacture or sale of products and services that cause environmental damage or health or safety hazards. We will inform our customers of the environmental impacts of our products or services and try to correct unsafe use.

Environmental Restoration. We will promptly and responsibly correct conditions we have caused that endanger health, safety or the environment. To the extent feasible, we will redress injuries we have caused to persons or damage we have caused to the environment and will restore the environment.

Informing the Public. We will inform in a timely manner everyone who may be affected by conditions caused by our company that might endanger health, safety or the environment. We will regularly seek advice and counsel through dialogue with persons in communities near our facilities. We will not take any action against employees for reporting dangerous incidents or conditions to management or to appropriate authorities.

Management Commitment. We will implement these principles and sustain a process that ensures that the Board of Directors and

Chief Executive Officers are fully informed about pertinent environmental issues and are fully responsible for environmental policy. In selecting our Board of Directors, we will consider demonstrated environmental commitment as a factor.

Audits and Reports. We will conduct an annual self-evaluation of our progress in implementing these principles. We will support the timely creation of generally accepted environmental audit procedures. We will annually complete the CERES report, which will be made available to the public.

The forty-eight companies, (including Coca-Cola, General Motors, Bank of America, Bethlehem Steel, and Polaroid) that have signed onto these CERES Principles, recognize that corporations must lead (rather than be led by government) the transition to a more ecologically sound economy. Companies that endorse these principles pledge to go voluntarily beyond the requirement of law. Lining up behind a similar effort are the auto and oil giants Ford, Chevron, Texaco and Shell, who are incorporating biodiversity principles into their operations.[132] All of these companies exemplify:

Eco-nomic Principle No. 8
Synergy Rules

In a fully evolved ecosystem, waste and pollution do not exist. What is waste to one species is food for another species. In a fully evolved economic system, what is one company's waste is another company's raw product material. Likewise, businesses that do not take advantage of green marketing, waste reduction, recycling, and energy efficiency will become the dead-end businesses of the new century. The new awakening in industry is about absorbing the lessons that should have been learned from nature long ago. Earth is in the hands of a more aware, enlightened species that has viewed Earth from a spacecraft. The hands-off approach to saving nature is not as effective as the hands-on approach. Proper use of the marketplace can accelerate the benefits back to the forests, mountains and oceans. Man and nature are forever entwined as they exist now. There is *no going back* to nature. There is only going forward together. Prosperity for humankind can, if done wisely and compassionately, be good for the environment.

Accepting this reality means that you are free to look for cooperative action or force. You are looking for synergy between capitalism and ecology. You are free to discover that green cuts both ways. Just as a greener economy helps nature, an economy reflecting natural principles of recycling, waste reduction and sustainability generates wealth. A key to finding this synergy is accepting profit as a justifiable motive for environmentally responsible actions.

It certainly wasn't difficult for David Beschen, a recycling entrepreneur in Preston, Washington, to accept the profit motive. "What drives me in making a difference in our world is making a profit," Beschen explains. "You hear a lot about sustainable futures. I can tell you what's sustainable—profit."[133] Pocketing greenbacks for green work, keeps the good going.

Today we even have environmentally correct mutual funds and money markets making a sustainable profit. Leaders in this field are the Calvert Social Investment Fund, Working Assets, Parnassus and Pax World—collectively managing billions in assets. Though these companies screen out many viable investments, i.e., no polluters, nuclear energy, or weapons builders, and thereby increase their risk, they often outperform the market. Pax World is one of the most successful—ranked 8th most profitable balanced fund for the year ending June 1998, according to *Kiplinger's Personal Finance*.[134] According to a study by the Social Investment Forum, assets in socially screened funds that include environmentally safe investments, surpassed $2 trillion in year 2000, a 36-percent increase in one year.[135] These mutual fund programs clearly show that profit and environmental responsibility are not mutually exclusive goals as we learned from many prominent companies and previously cited studies.

Another way of tapping into the profit motive is eco-labeling. Green labels are spreading from Europe to America and from laundry detergent to timber. The theory behind eco-labeling is simple. As you become more affluent or want to do more to protect the environment, you don't mind spending a few cents more for a sustainable product. A reliable, certifiable label helps you make the right choice environmentally. Eco-labels, while slow to catch on in the U.S., are hot in Europe, particularly Germany. Leading the U.S. into the green market is the timber industry through the work of the Forest Stewardship Council.

In 1993, 130 forestry and environmental representatives from around the world launched the Forest Stewardship Council (FSC). The Forest Stewardship Council is now seen as an independent, internationally credible body that has set standards by which forests and forest products can be managed and harvested in a sustainable, environmentally acceptable manner. The FSC initiative is centered on the appointment and accreditation of qualified certification bodies to inspect and evaluate forests in accordance with the FSC standards. With two certification bodies accredited in the U.S., the program is well underway in western forests.[136]

Collins Pine Co., a small timber company in northern California, which always had high stewardship principles, jumped at the opportunity to take the high ground. "The company felt it had to win back the public's trust, which had been lost in the fight over the spotted owl," explains Jim Quinn, president of Collins Pine. "As an industry we've got to work a lot harder to put that train back on track."[137]

Besides seeking the high ground and validation of their good forestry practices, Collins Pine Co. also hoped to gain a marketing advantage by having their stewardship signed off by approved certifiers. Collins Pine Co. scored well. In sustainability of timber resources, they received 86 out of 100 points. For maintenance of the forest ecosystem, they scored 81, and for socioeconomic benefits to the surrounding community, they scored 89.

Initially, buyers were passive due to the chain-of-custody requirements in the FSC program. However, Home Depot, a large retailer, was supportive of the certification initiative. Today Collins's shelving supplies are promoted in Home Depot stores throughout the San Francisco Bay Area. EcoTimber International, a Berkeley California lumber merchant, also features wood from Collins Pine Co. Aaron Maizlish, president of EcoTimber, notes that sales of certified wood increased fourfold in the past year (1997), and at $2 million, now accounts for two-thirds of his business.[138]

The largest certified forest in America is the 975,000-acre forest owned by Seven Islands Land Company in Bangor, Maine. "Green certification has been good for Seven Islands," says company president John Cashwell. "It provides access to markets that wouldn't otherwise exist. Seven Islands is expanding sales more widely around Europe, where the green campaign is far stronger. In the U.S. market, most observers contend that green certification is just a niche market. As more people learn about green certification, growth is expected."

"When I first offered green-certified wood, a lot of people said 'Ah that's b—,'" says Paul Fuge, owner of Plaza Hardwoods in New Mexico. "Now, it is being specified by architects."[139]

Currently, it is an open question whether or not eco-labels will become a major economic force in the U.S. "It's a very pure idea," says Phil Evans of Britain's Consumers Association. "The problems come in the actual practice."[140] Paper recycling, for example, in remote sparsely populated areas may consume more resources than it saves. Which is better: products meeting the eco-rules but made in a plant that dumps wastewater into sewage, or not-so-pure products made in a plant that treats its waste on site? These types of problems impede U.S. market receptivity for eco-labels. As U.S. corporations move their products into Europe where more of the market is eco-label sensitive, they too will change in response to the global nature of business. Anyway you look at it, eco-labeling is raising the consumer's consciousness about sustainable resources and should be viewed as a move in the right direction.

Banks are also growing in their appreciation for the effect of sustainability on their local and global foundation. One bank that stands out in this regard is Chicago's Shorebank Corporation. Shorebank is partnering with the community of Willapa Bay, Washington, to transform Willapa Bay into a more sustainable community. A third partner is EcoTrust, a foundation dedicated to conservation-based development in the coastal rainforest. Their challenge is to grow businesses while reducing waste and energy use, improve fishing, forestry, and farm practices, reduce use of chemicals and add value to goods and services in their communities.[141] To address this challenge, Shorebank has taken on the role of a holding company, a for-profit real estate company and a community-development nonprofit. "Shorebank's genius lies in its structure," says Ted Wolf of EcoTrust. "Shorebank realized it was not enough to open just a bank. It needed other credit resources."

In 1992, EcoTrust teamed up with the Chicago bank to form Willapa Bay's Shore Trust, "the first environmental bancorporation." The final affiliate will be a combination of a real estate company and a land trust. To help create demand for their products, a local trading group works to develop green markets for green products.[142] Although EcoTrust is pleased with the fit between Shorebank and Willapa Bay, it is too soon to declare a sustainable success. If Shorebank does succeed, it could change the way rural banks view lending opportunities. "ShoreTrust is trying to demonstrate an idea that's off the charts," exclaims Wolf.[143] Shorebank is acting on the synergy between market and community forces. Imagine this type of integrated structure—bank, real estate company, and community nonprofit—at work inside the World Bank. Instead of rural Washington, it is the Brazil rainforest.

Attempting to push this synergy envelope even further is the International Institute for Ecological Economics. The economists in this institute attempt to apply the principle of economic and ecological synergy at the World Bank and United Nations level. They explain the vision of ecological economics this way:

> As an open, dynamic subsystem of the overall, finite global ecosphere, the human population and its socio-economy is an integral part of the life-supporting environment, physically interconnected by the flows of energy and matter at various scales in time and space. The life support environment is the basis, and healthy ecosystems are a precondition for human welfare. Hence, the ecological economic worldview treats humans as *a part of and not apart from* the processes and function of nature.[144]

I read this as ecology is economy is ecology. If that's not enough global confirmation, I think about these words from a 1987 report of the World Commission on Environment and Development, the Brundtland Report:

> "We have become accustomed to a sharp increase in economic interdependence among nations. We are now forced to accustom ourselves to an accelerating ecological interdependence among nations. Ecology and economy are becoming more interwoven—locally, regionally, nationally, and globally—into a seamless net of causes and effects."[145]

Hence, the logo for eco-nomics:

CHAPTER 8

Navigating the Extremes

So are the local conservation society and the Chamber of Commerce in places like Ketchikan Alaska now holding hands singing "ecology is economy is ecology" to the tune of "Kumbayha My Lord"? Hardly. Even if you accept the argument that good business equals good environment and see the holistic vision of eco-nomics, this type of thinking is not yet common enough in our everyday world of politics. I can hear ex-pulp mill workers saying this is all just a lot of new-age hogwash. I can hear the words of a fellow Ketchikan Borough Assembly member, "Kate, I've been trying to tell you for years that the only thing in the middle of the road are yellow lines and skunks."

This reprimand about seeking and believing in common ground always stopped me cold. It has bothered me for years. So one day when crossing Tongass Avenue in Ketchikan Alaska, I literally checked out that middle of the road. I was prompted to pause and observe the road by the fact that an old nemesis of mine had stopped his vehicle to let me cross. (People in Ketchikan always stop for pedestrians.) So halfway across, I crouched down low, and you know what I found out? I discovered that the middle is the highest point in the road. It is also the part of the road less worn and traveled. I stood up, smiled at the timber lobbyist behind the wheel of the stopped car, crossed over to the harbor, and thought about these well-known lines of Robert Frost:

> I shall be telling this with a sigh
> Somewhere ages and ages hence:
> Two roads diverged in a wood, and I
> I took the one less traveled by,
> And that has made all the difference.

In other words, being in the middle—the part less traveled by—is not necessarily a symptom of indecision like a confused skunk. Yellow in the middle of the road does not mean cowardice; it means "no passing." It means "follow me for a while." Often the middle of the road is the only logical path for moving forward, and it takes courage to stick to it precisely because it is the part less traveled.

We need courage because it is often challenging to find the middle of the road through all the political potholes. Every rural community in the west shelters the voices of polarity somewhere, someway. As many of us know, these voices, once energized, can be quite influential. One must take a deep sigh and try to move forward through the potholes and seek the high ground whenever possible. One must accept these voices of polarity as the guardrails on each side of the road. They stake out the edges; the extreme points of view. Such views may be irreconcilable, but at least they define the debate and set the challenge for collaboration.

For example, here are two voices of polarity common to many environmental debates. These particular voices come from a one-person play entitled, *In the Heart of the Wood*.[146] In touring thirty towns in Washington and Oregon, this play, written by Todd Jefferson Moore, received much praise and critical acclaim. The voices of Ron and Andy represent the guardrails along Interstate 5, the highway that traverses the heart of spotted owl country:

Ron: This notion of sustainability is stupid. Grow or die! That's how the universe works! Sustainability? Okay. You got a 4-year-old girl. Feed her enough calories to sustain her at four years old and by the time she's five, she'll be dead. Because she needs more. We've got to grow. If your soul can't grow—and in the suffocating doom of environmentalism, your soul can't grow. The creative intent of the people who made the scientific and industrial revolution is what environmentalists deny. They cannot see it because they have not a creative bone in their body. All they can say is STOP!

Andy: Do I try to find common ground? Well, I don't, and my organization doesn't, and I think less of the environmental organizations that do. I see my job as an advocate for generations to come and for species that can't talk. It's my job to represent that view. It's my inherent faith in the system—so you see it's not my job (long pause) to compromise. It's not my job (pause) to solve all the world's problems. "Oo-oo-oo what are we going to do with these timber workers? What are we going to do with timber supply? And stuff like that. (Interruption) Excuse me."

With this kind of attitude, finding the middle of the road is hard. Helping to find the part of the road less traveled is the purpose behind the principles of eco-nomics. Use them as a road map. Treat the voices of polarity as the guardrails that define the outer limits of compromise. Andy and Ron will never join hands and sing Kumbayah together. Yet lots of other people representing the same affected interests just might.

To demonstrate that the potential exists to find the high ground of the middle, an exercise in mis-association is shown below. Match up the quotations on the following page with the correct source.

Quote	Source
1. "Encouraging industry to clean up its act is precisely the goal ___ sets out to achieve"	A. Article in <u>Good Housekeeping</u> Magazine
2. "Breaching four dams on the Lower Snake River makes economic sense and restores an Idaho treasure. If salmon return to the state in substantial numbers, which they will if the dams are breached, the long-term benefits outweigh any short term losses."	B. Chairman of the Northwest Indian Fisheries Commission
	C. EcoTrust
	D. Article in <u>Mother Jones</u> Magazine
3. "Most important of all, environmental laws and consumer preferences for non-polluting products have given rise to creative technologies needed to keep the U.S. competitive in the growing $370 billion world market for green goods and services."	E. Editor of <u>Idaho Statesman</u> Newspaper
	F. International Chamber of Commerce
4. "We at ___ believe that conservation must base its mission on a new approach, one that engages the forces of social and economic development..."	
5. "The future will likely belong to pro-active environmentalists, people who are able to use informatoin and technology, who don't mind living in this world as it is, and who are unafraid to engage in the hands-on management of ecosystems."	
6. "Every time you turn on a light bulb, a salmon smolt flies out. We're not going to turn out the lights and we're not going to stop using trees. But there is a right way to do these things."	

147 148 149 150 151 152

How did you do? Were you surprised? Even if you matched them up fairly well, I hope this exercise reminded you of that old adage, "You shouldn't judge a book by its cover." You may find like-minded, open, eco-nomic allies in corners you don't expect; particularly if you start with Eco-nomic Principle No. 1—Conservation Is a Universal Value.

If accepting conservation as a universal value is one starting point where you might find a reasonable, like-minded person, another lies in changing perspectives about prosperity and growth. Many people now believe that uncontrolled progress has its flaws. In the eloquent words of Edward Abbey, "Growth for the sake of growth is the ideology of cancer." While these words first espoused in the 1960s were tantamount to capitalistic treason, the accomplishments of the environmental movement since then now give Abbey's words an echo of truth for many of us. Endless growth on a finite planet has been exposed as fantasy.

"Growth for the sake of growth" has been replaced with the paradigm of "sustainable development," which simply means meeting the needs of communities so that resources can be sustained for future generations. Accepting these starting points changes the debate from who really cares about conservation or who really cares about growth to who really cares about how we manage nature for the sake of man and nature.

Wallace Kaufman, president of two state-level environmental groups in North Carolina, explains the new environmental debate this way:

> "The debate in our society is not really between those who care about nature and those who do not. Everyone has a preferred environment. Less than half of one percent of the world really wants to live in a wilderness, or even in a cabin at Walden Pond. The debate is over how to manage nature for human purposes. How do we keep the oceans supplying us with fish? How do we keep the atmosphere from reacting too extremely to our use of oil, gas and aerosols? We know how to preserve grizzly bears, pandas, elephants, and rhinos, but we have to ask if we really want them. Since we have surrounded their habitats with our own civilization, there is no returning the decision to nature. It is up to us to decide whether they starve to death, get killed by poachers, or are managed by the most scientific and humane methods we have."[153]

It is up to us. Again I ask: Are we willing to trust our knowledge and insights to do right by man and nature to practice ecosystem management and sustainable development, knowing that change is often unpredictable? If we answer yes, then we can move beyond the starting points and enter the deeper debate on how to manage in the most scientific and humane way possible.

However, entering this debate on science and human impact also invites extreme points of view. At one end is the anti-environment rhetoric that reduces all scientific reports from the environmental community to the "crisis-of-the month" membership ploy. At the other end is the quick, tainted dismissal of environmental concerns from industry. The authors of *Eco-Sanity* argue that the environmental movement has become a victim of its own success:

> "Having delivered the message of impending doom for decades it knows no other strategy. Many environmental crises are simply manufactured out of flimsy evidence and marketing puffery. As a result, the three highest priorities of the environmental movement during the 1980s and 1990s—global warming, ozone depletion, and acid rain— each lacked solid scientific evidence of significant harm to either plant or animal life."[154]

The authors of *Eco-Sanity* are not alone in this view. Four out of ten Americans surveyed said, "Environmental activist groups exaggerate the environmental threats facing our planet in order to gain public attention."[155] Four out of five business executives and six out of ten Congressional staffers believe that environmental extremists will take advantage of public fears in order to pursue their own agendas.[156]

At the other end, Anne and Paul Ehrlich, authors of *Betrayal of Science and Reason*, argue that groups like the Wise Use Movement systematically set out to undermine and misinterpret environmental data. The authors call this tactic anti-science or "brownlash."

The anti-science brownlash provides a rationalization for these short-term perspectives: Old-growth forests are decadent and should be harvested; extinction is natural, so there's no harm overharvesting economically important animals; there is abundant undisturbed habitat so human beings have a right to develop land anywhere and in any way they choose; global warming is a hoax or even will benefit agriculture; and so on.[157] This thinking does not address, let alone resolve, serious environmental problems.

Like so many issues, the scientific truth concerning environmental issues lies somewhere in the middle between "crisis of the month" rhetoric and "brownlash." In navigating between these extremes I find it helpful to understand the difference between ecology and environmentalism. Ecology is a science. It produces knowledge. Environmentalism, like the "wise use" crusade, is a political movement. It produces action and laws. Political movements rely on advocacy journalism. Science relies on peer-review reporting.

Going back to my own personal experience. My undergraduate major was in ecology. After doing a definitive paper on the ecology of a salamander found in Iowa, I realized that I didn't just want to produce scientific reports. I wanted to be the person who pulled the ecological reports off the shelf to produce tangible results. As such, I went on to study natural resource management. Driven by the desire for action and change, I eventually found myself immersed in resource politics. I soon learned that to achieve ecological goals, political movements are indispensable for achieving action, but those same movements may, through the political process, obscure the goals and objectives defined by ecologists. At the risk of overgeneralizing, ecologists tend to recommend a "hands-on" approach as opposed to the "hands-off" approach often advocated by crisis-motivated environmentalists. While not all ecologists will agree about the best way to proceed, science-based decision-making is a lot closer to the truth. I have learned to seek ecological validation of the environmental issue at hand. It exists. One just has to dig below the rhetoric.

Another rhetoric flash point that one must be wary of is

the conflict between habitat protection and private property. Environmentalists who see property rights activists as greedy landowners and as shields for big business have too simplistic a view of the issue. Likewise, property rights activists who label any criticism of how they manage their land as communism miss the point completely. As I was taught in my first class on natural resource economics, land ownership is not a legal rock where you own every possible right to your property. It is like a bundle of sticks, a bundle of rights. Some you hold, some you do not. For example, the right to build a supermarket in a residential district has been removed by zoning. Often the right to exclude public services is held in check by public easements and rights of way. The catch is that these limitations of rights are established before purchase and reflected in the price paid for the land. Rights removed later for public purposes are to be compensated for, according to our U.S. Constitution.

The property rights or takings controversy is not about rights long gone or voluntarily relinquished through the marketplace; it's about rights taken by government without just compensation. Labeling the controversy as "greed" or "communism" is a shallow attempt not to address the real issue of just compensation. Environmental leader Wallace Kaufman gets at this real issue of property rights:

> "It is well and good and scientifically sound to say that preserving the red-cockaded woodpecker, the grizzly bear, the wolves, clear water, or the acid balance of a lake protects the environmental that supports us all, but it is also true that private property rights sustain us all, including the freedom we have to be environmental activists. To take a valuable right without paying does not seem very different to the owner than if the government singled him out for a special individualized tax to save the red-cockaded woodpecker or a canoeist's view of the New River's banks. Environmentalists like to argue that what landowners lose is eventually

compensated for by a healthier economy and other public benefits. Perhaps, but why are a few individuals chosen to make sacrifices to improve life for everyone else?"[158]

Oregon residents felt strongly enough about this issue of compensation that they put the question to a vote in the 2000 election. Voters in Oregon approved a measure to require compensation of property owners from state regulations that reduce land value. It's interesting to see this vote occur in a state, which is considered to be an environmentally progressive state.

The Oregon vote as well as the words of Wallace Kaufman reminds us that we are all in this sustainable, biodiversity quest together. Affected public and private interests must share the burden of responsibility and fairness alike. Deciding how to equitably share this responsibility is a difficult task. But we must first begin by acknowledging the legitimate property rights of others.

In navigating the extremes, I have talked about treating the rhetoric exemplified by Ron and Andy as the guardrails that frame one's search for the higher middle ground. Well beyond the guardrails, on into the abyss, is the act of violence against property or person. There is simply no place for violence.

Mainstream environmental organizations denounce the Earth First! tactic of spiking trees with large nails dangerous to an unsuspecting logger. These same organizations along with Earth First! strongly condemn the eco-terrorists activities of the Earth Liberation Front (ELF). There is no room in the court of public opinion for actions like ELF's burning down of restaurants and ski lifts at Vail, Colorado. As noted in the *Denver Post* and repeated in editorials across the nation: "The tactics of radical outfits like ELF are a disservice to the mainstream environmental movement. Calling for violence crosses the boundaries of what is acceptable in an open society."[159] Furthermore, it makes no sense to destroy the environment in a cause to save the environment. Where is the sense in that?

Unfortunately, arson as a tactic is not limited to one side. David

Helvarg, in his book *The War Against the Greens*, factually details several accounts where the homes of environmentalists were burned by anti-environment forces. And the violence is not limited to arson. Helvarg, a veteran journalist and private investigator, concludes:

> "Along with the growth of Wise Use/Property Rights, the last nine years (1985-94) have seen a startling increase in intimidation, vandalism, and violence directed against grassroots environmental activists. Observers of this trend have documented hundreds of acts of violence, ranging from vandalism, assaults, arson, and shootings to torture, rape and possibly murder, much of it occurring in rural and low-income communities."[160]

Acts of terrorism, just like in the Mideast, obviously serve to shut down the dialogue and prolong the war. These acts lie in the abyss and the only way to deal with them is through zero tolerance. There is no navigating violent acts because there is no place for violence.

Name-calling, however counterproductive it may be, is a far better outlet for extreme viewpoints. At least through time and integrity, the negative effect of name-calling can be worn down. This, I have learned through observing and knowing former Republican Governor of Alaska Jay Hammond. During his tenure he was accused of everything, from insurrection to insanity. For example, when he introduced a resolution asking for an economic evaluation of an alternative oil pipeline route, he was labeled, "anti-Alaskan, anti-American, anti-development, anti-business, and that ultimate of all denunciation in the [Anchorage] *Times*' lexicon, "environmental preservationist!"[161] Since then, events and a reputation as Alaska's favorite statesman have given all this misplaced name-calling of Governor Hammond a very hollow ring.

While environmental name-calling may no longer stick to statesmen like Governor Hammond, it remains a favorite pastime in many areas and is particularly common during the election season. Less common is the use of humor to defuse acrimony and polarity. My only experience in this area comes from a pie-throwing contest, where the opposing sides bid on the right to throw a pie at their chosen arch nemesis, and the proceeds went to supporting college scholarships. The event took place in the middle of a five-day meeting on a hot, divisive fish topic. The laughing together afterwards was just as intense as the hoots and chants during the actual pie toss. More importantly, the discussion the next day seemed more civil and productive. While there was not any singing in the aisle when the final vote came, this nonetheless taught me not to underestimate the value of humor when navigating the extremes.

Then there is the idea of having a male modeling contest between the "Hunks for Habitat" and the "Studs for Timber." Hmm, maybe even the Ketchikan Chamber of Commerce would go for this idea sometime.

(Answers for quote match on page 113: 1F, 2E, 3A, 4C, 5D, 6B)

CHAPTER 9

Leadership That Says 'Yes' to Eco-nomics

Robert Frost once said, "An idea is a feat of association." To advance the idea of eco-nomics, I aim to associate this idea with similar ideas advanced by more recognized leaders. Perhaps by association with leadership, eco-nomics will be seen as an idea whose time has come. While this chapter mixes in quotations of a few prominent politicians and businessmen, it relies on three distinct and unique leaders: one a Governor, one an environmentalist and one an economist. Although none of these leaders have, per se, signed on to the principles of eco-nomics as articulated in the previous chapters, they all espouse a vision of linkage between the environment and the economy.

Let's start with former Republican Governor of Alaska, Jay Hammond. Despite the anti-growth label that his Democrat opponent put on him, Jay Hammond was first elected as Governor in 1974 and served until 1982. Why pay attention to this past Governor of Alaska? First, as I stated on page fourteen, "development versus environment," conflicts are easily triggered in Alaska and Hammond was in the middle of many of these conflicts. Secondly, Hammond was involved in the politics surrounding the construction of the Alaska oil pipeline. His message resonates even louder today given the wreck of the *Exxon Valdez* on Bligh Reef. Thirdly, Hammond is an uncommon politician. As a self-described "Bush Rat Governor," he speaks with refreshing honesty about himself and the predatory nature of resource politics. Take for example this excerpt from his book *Tales of Alaska's Bush Rat Governor* (amplified by recent interview notes):

"Empathizing a bit with both factions, often I placed a foot in each camp, only to find I'd stepped into a campfire. As Governor, I put all development proposals up against three criteria: 1) is it environmentally sound, 2) is it a good business deal for the people in general or just for a select few, and 3) do the people want it given all the costs. And I declared that if a project meets these criteria, I'll support it and if it doesn't, I'll oppose it. Well initially, when I made these statements, the environmentalist only heard support. On the other hand, the Chamber of Commerce development types only heard that I would oppose it.

Only after much punishment did I learn that more astute politicians ponder such questions in private. Until I learned this lesson, opponents happily bombed me with charges of inconsistency. Although I might be in accord with them 90 percent of the time, that 10-percent deviation enraged extremists on both sides. Some conservationists believed I should do all in my power to stifle growth and development; some developers were certain I aspired to zero growth and would return Alaska to a howling wilderness.[162]

One project that Hammond put up against his three criteria was the Alaska oil pipeline. Using these criteria, he came to the conclusion that the route through Canada made more sense from both the environmental and economic standpoint than the all-Alaska route. In his own words:

"Clearly, Alaska would experience far less environmental trauma with only six hundred overland miles of pipeline construction across its wilderness than nine hundred miles to Valdez—not to mention the pollution hazards of tankering via Prince William Sound and down the Pacific Coast. The fact that the planned pipeline terminal at Valdez would be erected on a major earthquake fault was also not mentioned, as I recall. In any event, transporting our oil through a single 2,100-mile trans-Canada line to the Midwest would clearly be less costly than tankering past West Coast ports—which is precisely what happened when the southern pipeline fell through and inadequate West Coast refining capacity required North Slope crude to be shipped to the Panama Canal. If there has ever been a greater waste of energy and economic potential than what Alaska and the nation paid for the all-Alaska pipeline route, I don't know what it might be."[163]

Long before the *Exxon Valdez* oil spill, Governor Hammond concluded that the environmental and economic analysis favored the trans-Canada route. However, the analysis didn't matter. The Alaskan labor unions hungry for construction contracts won the day in the court of the *Anchorage Times*. As Hammond explains, "Almost no one in Alaska, save of course preservationists extremists, dared suggest we even *look* at a Canadian route for fear of being branded a crackpot conservationist like Hammond by the state's most powerful newspaper and labor unions."

Now, with the high ecological and economic cost of the *Exxon Valdez*, Hammond takes little solace in the fact that more and more people say we should have gone through Canada. Instead, he hopes that the lessons of hindsight will help Alaska move forward; help Alaskans see the value of merging economic and environmental values. In the closing chapter of his autobiography entitled, "Wither Alaska?" he writes:

> "To developers, I said Alaska's long-term economic health depends on a healthy environment. To environmentalists, I said, 'You can more likely derail projects that threaten quality of life by holding growth proponents' feet to the fire on the economic self-interest of Alaskans than you can by fanning flames of environmentalism.' Folk who couldn't care less about dicky birds will sit up and take notice of some economic

turkey that pecks at their pocket books. I am convinced that only through an amalgam of economics and environmentalism can Alaska hope to sustain values which make this the place most of us wish to live."[164]

As stated above, for Governor Hammond, the *Exxon Valdez* oil spill was unwanted vindication that he was right to have economically and environmentally questioned the all-Alaska route. For some economists and political leaders, the *Exxon Valdez* was further verification that our economic system of measuring productivity is flawed. As vice-president Al Gore points out in his book *Earth in the Balance*, our most basic measure of economic performance, the gross national product (GNP), does not measure resource depreciation and ignores the cost of clean air and water, and as such, the *Exxon Valdez* spill actually increased our GNP.[165]

To offset this economic blindness to environmental costs, Vice-President Gore recommends at least changing the calculation of productivity enough to include those economic impacts of pollution for which we have an accepted value, such as the $4 billion cost of cleaning up the spill in Prince William Sound. The oil spill should be counted as a loss and not a gain in productivity.

For many environmental leaders like vice-president Gore, this failure to account for all the resource costs of development and production imposes a fundamental obstacle to ever securing complete integration of our economic and environmental systems. Denis Hayes, a major environmental leader, agrees, but he sees more to the equation. Hayes is best known for making Earth Day 1970 a monumental event. As President of $100 million Bullitt Foundation, he now focuses on supporting sustainable development projects in the Pacific Northwest. Showing both a passionate eco-advocate side and a credible pragmatic side, the Seattle press has dubbed him "The Great Green Hope." He also serves as Chair of the Energy Foundation in San Francisco and co-chairs the Coalition for Environmentally Responsible Economies. For Hayes, although the external cost of pollution and degradation is important, it's only one-half of the equation for market-generated environmental reform. The other half is being price competitive. Based on his vast experience in utilities, Hayes believes that making environmentally preferred products or services price competitive is achievable with the assistance of government.

In a personal interview, Hayes explains his approach to economic and environmental integration this way:

> "If you get the prices wrong, everything else that you do [to foster environmental change] is a second order effect. You have to get the prices right . . . making it less expensive to do the right thing and more expensive to do the wrong thing. If you want to do something about global warming, then you must get some kind of a shadow price to carbon dioxide emissions, such as a carbon tax. Unless you pass revenue-neutral pollution taxes, you won't get past the 'sucker for a cheap deal' mentality. Besides, why should it cost more do the right thing? Why ask consumers to act against their own perceived best interests? When it comes to choosing electricity, people would rather have a law banning the more harmful but cheaper energy than be given a choice of paying a few cents more per kilowatt-hour for green electricity. Why make the sacrifice when others get by with less and little difference is made in terms of the environment? People expect to make selfless sacrifices in church, but not in a department store. We must change this sacrifice expectation around and get the price right. When it is in the manufacturer's interest and the consumer's interest to do things right, they will be motivated to do what is right."[166]

Bill Ford Jr., the new President of Ford Motor Company and a recognized environmentalist, agrees with Hayes about the need to overcome the sacrifice aspect of new technology. "Regular drivers won't buy high-tech clean cars until the industry has a 'no-tradeoff vehicle' that performs just as well as a gasoline vehicle at the same price," proclaims Ford.[167] To create such a car, Ford and other carmakers are getting some high-powered help through government research and technology transfer. This is consistent with Denis Hayes' approach to solving today's environmental problems.

While Hayes embraces a dominant role for the marketplace in fostering environmental change, he still sees the need for the strong guiding hand of government through technology assistance, economic incentives and proper tax and subsidy structures to help get the price right. He also favors a non-proscriptive regulatory framework to overcome the economic stickiness caused by corporate inertia and short-term thinking.

This reliance on government became particularly evident when I asked him to reflect back on the "doom and gloom" predictions that emanated from the environmental movement in the 1960s and 1970s. What of the full-scale catastrophes that never happened? Is this due in part to underestimating man's creative capacity?

Hayes: "You have heard of self-fulfilling prophecies. The environmental predictions of the 1960s were self-undoing prophecies. We caused society to see where it was heading, and it changed direction. Sure the prediction in *Silent Spring* did not materialize; we banned DDT. The same for the Federation of Atomic Scientists; we banned atmospheric nuclear testing. The same for my own claims about poisonous urban air; we passed the Clean Air Act. The same for urban sewage and flammable rivers; we passed the Clean Water Act. To the extent that human creativity came into play, it was not just a spontaneous blooming. It was triggered in very large part by the environmental movement's success in changing the rules by which corporate decisions were made. Companies were not evil in 1969 and virtuous in 1974. They just faced a new set of boundary conditions imposed by the Clean Air Act, the Clean Water Act, the Resource Conservation and Recovery Act, Superfund, the Endangered Species Act, the Forest Protection Act, the Occupational Health and Safety Act, and the need to file Environmental Impact Statements—NONE of which existed in 1969! We predicted calamities by extrapolating then-current trends;

we mobilized heroic forces to change society's direction; we thus avoided the calamities."[168]

Moving from looking back to looking forward for the environmental movement, Hayes clearly sees a shift from relying on government to set the "No" boundaries on corporations to finding ways to say "Yes." "The environmental movement has been enormously successful in saying no, in saying what people and companies cannot do," notes Hayes. "But we have seldom committed ourselves to a positive vision of things that people can do, of what can be achieved, of basically, saying yes."[169] And as President of the Bullitt Foundation, he says "Yes" with funds for community-oriented sustainable development projects in the Pacific Northwest. He also uses his President's seat to pitch many "Yes" energy ideas. For example, he advocates a $5 billion federal program to buy solar cells. Given what the Defense Department and NASA procurement did for the computer chip—making prices fall and creating an explosive market—he sees the same parallel opportunity for the solar cell.

"We should provide a subsidy that the solar cell industry can only earn by drastically lowering the price of its products. As soon as solar technology crosses the price barrier, sales will explode—like television or cellular phones," he writes in his 1997 President's Report for the Bullitt Foundation.[170] The organizer of Earth Day 2000 is setting a poignant example for change within the environmental movement—from setting the "No" boundaries to seeking the "Yes" ways of community activism and in harnessing the power of the marketplace.

Another environmental leader seeking new "Yes" ways was EPA Administrator Carol Browner. Called "a new type of environmentalist" by *The New York Times*, Browner viewed economic development and environmental protection as complementary goals. She viewed her Common Sense Initiative as a clear example of how regulatory reform can aid industry and the environment at the same time. By taking an industry-by-industry approach to regulation, the abilities of regulators to take a comprehensive approach to air, water, soil, and toxic pollution was greatly improved. As she directed her staff, "Let's measure our success not by how many rules we adopt but by whether a specific industry can achieve environmental protection cleaner, cheaper, and smarter." Her Common Sense Initiative also directed a change in the agency's views toward technology. Rather than telling each industry what technology to use to meet a particular standard, regulators are now directed to encourage new technology. "Why not encourage creativity and innovation?" asked Browner. "The results will be that not only will we meet new standards—we will exceed the standards and achieve true pollution prevention."[171]

This approach by Browner recognized that the dialogue has changed inside corporate boardrooms; that stockholders pay attention to the company policies on environmental management and pollution controls. As referenced in chapter six, this is a theme close to the message of economist Michael Silverstein. In addition to publishing *The Environmental Economic Revolution*, Mr. Silverstein teaches at the Management Institute of New York University and writes regular columns for business magazines. He sees this dialogue about pollution abatement as becoming institutionalized. In a personal interview in January 1998, Silverstein elaborated:

> "I consider a green economy to be synonymous with an evolving high-tech economy. If we get a lot of garbage coming out of smokestacks then basically we're in economic adolescence. The need for environmental protection just hastens the transformation to a less-wasteful and less-polluting economy. It's a synergism at work here."[172]

The debate over environment versus jobs completely misses this synergism. So does the talk of finding balance. As Vice President Al Gore says, "The key is not merely to balance the twin goals of economic growth and environmental protection, but to connect them—and to do so through innovation."[173] Here again, Bill Ford is leading by example. When the chairman of Ford Motor Co. decided to rebuild a historic plant destroyed by an explosion in 1999, he set out to make the new plant as environmentally friendly as possible while being fiscally responsible. Thirty-five skylights and an ivy-covered roof later, he is about to open a 2.1 million-square-foot factory at a savings of $35 million in construction and energy costs.[174]

Finding balance, while still a desirable goal, conveys a trading off, a weighing of concerns and consequences. It does not denote this connection that Silverstein and Gore speak of, nor does it adequately capture the results being produced by CEO's like Bill Ford. This leads Silverstein to believe we have a problem with language:

> "Language, as well as history, has long muddied the environmental economic debate. Indeed one of the chief reasons people can still even speak of choosing between the environment and the economy is that they are ascribing meaning to certain key words and terms that are decades out of date. Growth, in other words, has taken on an entirely different relationship to the environment in our own time. Nineteenth-century, pollution-based growth was environmentally unsound and inherently unsustainable. Late-twentieth-century growth is far more environmentally sensitized and, for that reason (at least in theory), infinitely sustainable. Think of any product in terms of its material content. In terms of its capability to be recycled, virtually everything is moving in the right direction. We have a greening economy being talked about in terms and language that doesn't fit."[175]

Perhaps updating the concept of growth would help those like Governor Hammond avoid the anti-growth label. To some extent this is what quality of life is. For Silverstein, this wasn't enough. He coined his own term—enomics—to capture the study of the linkage between the health of the world's ecosystems and the wealth of the world economies. Looking just within the boardrooms of corporate America to find forces of linkage, he attributes linkage to these enomic forces:

1) The pervasive effects of a true-world marketplace in which there is a far greater need for efficient technologies and management techniques to meet far stronger international competition.
2) The emergence of a potent green buying preference within key sectors of this international marketplace.
3) A dawning realization that government and corporate spending on environmental protection and restoration, over and above the spending generated by individuals' green-buying preferences, has the potential to create a mammoth new set of business opportunities.

Silverstein acknowledges that part in parcel to these forces acting in the marketplace is the emergence of stronger regulations designed to protect the world's ecosystems. Again seeing the synergy of forces. "Basically all modern economies naturally gravitate toward a greener configuration," proclaims Silverstein. His belief in this trend is so strong that he takes a different view from Al Gore and Denis Hayes on the subject of accounting for external development costs. Silverstein thinks that accounting for externalities are too "fuzzy" and that the efforts to account for the health cost of bad air or for the impact costs of polluted waters will only slow the greening process down. "You can make external costs into anything you want," explains Silverstein. Based on his research into the growing environmental awareness of corporations, Silverstein believes that accounting of external costs is not necessary to make a case for good environmental policies. "For most corporations there are very good reasons to deal with environmental issues. There is almost always a good case to make, whether it is accommodating customers and shareholders, preserving community good will, or using fuel with a longer term use." So if accounting for externalities is not necessary to prod good environmental practices within corporate America, Silverstein believes that the discussion is moot and becomes a distraction.[176]

This very brief discussion on external costs points out that there is not complete agreement on the details of how best to foster the integration of the economic and ecological systems with the world's economies. Nor is there consensus on the specifics for the government's new environmental role. Nonetheless, it is important to note that the dialogue of disagreement has shifted from "environment versus economy" to how best to merge these dominant forces in our lives. The question is no longer one of prompting or deciding to be environmentally responsible; it is now one of how to define and accelerate that responsibility through the use of government and economic forces.

I feel an eco-nomic shift going on. I feel the presence of prominent company on the road less traveled. I even feel connected to a well-established bank president, Roswell King Milling, who now travels the state of Louisiana championing the need to save the wetlands. He preaches this message to the state's powerbrokers: "The environment is the economy."[177]

CHAPTER 10

Think Local—Act Global

A grand day in paradise. Tuned by Beethoven's Fifth Symphony, I skied into grandeur today at the base of the Mendenhall Glacier. It's warm, no wind, no clouds. Just blue sky and sun. All around there is nothing but sunshine smiling my way. I ski around icebergs masquerading as blue castles. I venture near cascading waterfalls frozen in art. On the headset, I play Beethoven's Fifth for the majesty of the mountains and eagles. T' is a perfect fit. Beethoven and mountains. With a music-induced sense of harmony between man and nature, I ski my knees and heart out on this glorious day. I get all my senses of joy renewed on outings like this. I feel privileged to bask in such beauty alone.

Just as I am alone this February morning, the first to ski in just-set tracks of glacier grandeur, I am alone in setting eco-nomic tracks into the ANWR (pronounced an-WAR) debate. At least I feel all alone. There is no environmental group or chamber that I know of that has quite the same take on opening a small portion of the Arctic National Wildlife Refuge (ANWR) to oil development. As I know from experiencing many splendid days at the glacier, it is a privilege to be alone in the wilderness of nature. But what about the wilderness of man—national politics. Is it a privilege to be alone on the issue of ANWR? No, not all. Instead, I feel like I am about to wade into quicksand with no one around to help pull me out.

As you may know, ANWR is a highly politicized issue. The "politics" here are extremely messy and polarized. There's no wading in without mud sticking to you or sand shifting below you. ANWR is the "Mideast" of environmental issues—fully charged with half-truths. As Senator Olympia Snowe acknowledges, "We're all consumed with the political aspects of the debate instead of the policy."[178]

Wading into the ANWR debate reminds me of the time I had no choice but to get involved in a volatile, fishermen strike. As the Executive Director of a fishermen's organization, I had no choice but to weigh in, albeit strikes were not listed in my job description. With much hesitation, I entered the fray knowing full well that all strain and strife would be my constant companion for the next week. A fisherman considered by many young skippers to be a "fleet father" counseled me then. He took me aside and spoke in his deep John Wayne voice, "Kate, you're doing the right thing to get involved. You can't duck it, but it's a matter of time until you step in shit. You can't avoid it on an issue like this. Just go in knowing that and let me know when it gets waist high." I did indeed step in it and I sunk up to my neck. Thanks to several "fleet fathers," I survived. So here I go again wading in and waiting for when I step in it. Only this time, there is no fleet father to catch me when I do. There is only the solace of place. I ski an extra loop along the face of the glacier. I hear the groan of centuries. I place my splayed hand upon the force that carves mountains. An eagle with sun on the wing soars overhead. I am privileged in my aloneness here. It's okay; I too can be alone in the wilderness of politics.

As an Alaskan, I have deeply mixed feelings about opening a small portion of the Arctic National Wildlife Refuge. To start, I've kayaked past the Gates of the Arctic, which is just outside ANWR. I've experienced the joy of basking with friends in the land of the midnight sun. I've marveled at the immensity of a landscape powerful enough to evoke images, twenty years later, of treeless, rocky peaks wrapped in carpets of turning tundra. While I have not experienced the thundering of thousands upon thousands of caribou migrating across the arctic tundra, I can still smile in appreciation for the grandeur of American wildness that these massive herds represent. To this day whenever I get into deep wilderness, my soul still travels to the awesome Arctic. And as such, I am drawn to the pleas of the environmental community to not touch "America's Sergenti".

However, when I consider that the potential oil production from ANWR equates to anywhere from 6 months to a year's oil supply for the United States, ANWR becomes much more than an oil, caribou and wilderness issue. It is really an energy policy debate. Can we do with less oil in our lives? Probably. Do I do as much as I can to wean myself of oil? Probably not. I could use my wood stove more. I do walk and bike to work but I still use gas to get away for the weekends and to do my shopping. I recycle all the plastic that I can. Still, I don't do enough and neither does our country. We as a "society on the move" are far too dependent on our daily oil fixes. In one way or another, we are all connected and perhaps conflicted by the issue of oil and the arctic (Prudhoe Bay makes up approximately 25 percent of U.S. oil production). To some degree it's like being conflicted between logging and the wood in my house, between industrialized farming and the fresh food in my refrigerator. Conflict or not, we do know that if managed *Right*, in the capital sense of the word, we can extract resources from wild places of beauty. Even President Jimmy Carter agrees, "Can you protect the beauty of God's work and still take care of the daily needs of people? . . . yes."[179]

Regardless of the comfort of these words, I can only resolve my oil-based lifestyle with my spiritual appreciation for the arctic wilderness if I think long-term and more globally. From the environmental and economic standpoint, there is a lot wrong with our current energy policy. To start, the Natural Resources Defense Council notes that we could save 15 times more oil than the refuge is likely to produce just by raising the average gas mileage of U.S. vehicles to 40 mpg by the year 2012. Yet, Congress moves in the opposite direction, exempting SUV and trucks from tougher mileage standards.

Unlike exemptions for SUVs, the Energy Policy Act languishes in committee inaction. The Energy Policy Act would:

- improve automobile fuel economy standards to 35 miles per gallon by 2013;
- provide incentives for consumers to purchase advanced gasoline-electric hybrid and fuel cell-powered vehicles;
- offer incentives for power companies to tap more renewable energy sources like wind and solar, and for builders to improve the energy efficiency of homes and offices;
- require retail electricity suppliers to purchase 10 percent of their electricity from renewable energy sources by 2020.[180] (Note: the European Union has set its goal for electricity from renewable sources to 22 percent within the next eight years.[181])

Instead of timely action on this legislation, the administration's energy plan focuses more on oil production and imports. Critics claim that the administration's policy makes us more dependent on foreign oil in 2020 than we are today and would increase global-warming pollution more than 30 percent. As noted in a letter signed by attorney generals from eleven states, "Far from proposing solutions to the climate change problem, the administration has been adopting energy policies that would actually increase greenhouse gas emissions".[182] These attorney generals are not alone in their assessment of the administration's policy on oil and global warming. In a poll conducted by the *Los Angeles Times* in April 2001, a majority of Americans supported the Kyoto Protocol on global warming. Yet, we move in the wrong direction on what is considered, even by mainstream Republicans, to be our most pressing environmental problem—global warming and climate change.

Why is this? Again it comes to the perceived loss of jobs. According to Christine Todd Whitman, EPA Administrator for the Bush administration, "Kyoto would put millions of Americans out of work for the sake of meeting unrealistic targets."[183] And jobs are behind the push for opening ANWR. Pitching the president's energy agenda, Secretary Gale Norton says that oil drilling in ANWR would produce 700,000 jobs. Environmentalists vehemently dispute this number and they claim a more accurate number is about 50,000. In the middle is a separate study convened by the Energy Department that estimates about a third as many jobs.[184] Rather than get into an analysis of the assumptions behind these job estimates, let's, for the sake of argument, accept the Energy Department figure that opening ANWR to oil development would create about 250,000 jobs. How does this compare with job estimates for a program committed to renewable energy and technologies fostering lower mpg and efficiencies?

A recent study by the Tellus Institute and MRG & Associates estimates that implementing a comprehensive package of clean energy policies and achieving efficiency improvements in the transport sectors would yield a net employment increase of 700,000 jobs in 2010, rising to more than one million by 2020.[185] These job estimates are built upon the assumption that 20 percent of electricity would come from wind, solar and geothermal by 2020. The researchers also assumed oil consumption would decline by approximately 8 percent between 2000 and 2020. Though these assumptions are optimistic, the results still allow one to compare job generation from ANWR (250,000 jobs) to the scale of jobs potentially available from a national commitment to a clean energy policy (700,000).

In this context and from the long-term jobs perspective, ANWR loses. From the long-term environment perspective, global warming continues to be ignored. But if the agendas are broad and linked, both can win in the long-term. Hence, to the ANWR debate I dedicate:

Eco-nomic Principle No. 9
Take the Long View Home

Whenever possible, define the issue in as global a context as possible. Also, define the time horizon for accountability long enough to allow for the economic benefits of alternative design and mitigation to be counted for in the equation of jobs and the environment. Think as far down the line as the dynamics of the issue allows. The longer the horizon, the larger the window for finding and promoting synergy. And always keep within the notion of being a global citizen. Seize the opportunity to enlarge the debate both in time and scope. Cross over to the middle of the road and take the long view home when position and timing give you the chance to define the context of the debate.

This is a very tough principle to carry out since the long-term length of our political perspective is often defined by the duration of elected office, which is two to six years. This is a far cry from the seven-generation rule of the Sioux Indians. Acting on this principle requires vision and statesmanship, both of which are commonly in short supply.

In lieu of having an administration to embolden this principle in regards to the ANWR debate, the challenge is how do we get an old-school administration to move toward a more sustainable energy economy? Now the politician in me comes forward. I ask what energy issue is it that the Bush administration appears willing to fall on their sword over? ANWR of course. In exchange for getting serious about global warming and renewable energy, can we not draw upon our experience with oil development in other refuges or in other similar environments to allow a modest area, say 2,000 acres, to be opened? If we entertain this question then the next set of questions comes back to the more local issues of resource compatibility, minimizing impacts, design and technology etc.

Unfortunately, the high profile, national polarization of the ANWR debate does not allow for such a question to be asked, let alone seriously explored. As many of you know, protecting ANWR is *the* postcard issue for hundreds of environmental groups. Protecting ANWR against oil development is a top priority of many of America's most influential environmental organizations. And similarly entrenched is the Bush administration. The lines are already drawn and they're drawn deep and hard. We even have "war" in the acronym. The parties are too poised for battle and as discussed in chapter five, it is important to know when a resource issue is ripe for resolution. ANWR is not ripe, nor is the scale of the debate broad enough to allow for any possible synergistic solution.

But let's suppose I were queen of environmental policy and could wave my magic wand to make ANWR ripe for resolution, what would I do? Within the framework of a legislatively bound commitment to:
1) work on fixing the Kyoto Protocol so that the work of 160 nations is not summarily dismissed;
2) secure the passage of the Energy Policy Act (see p. 185) and;
3) explore and extract oil in an "environmentally responsible" manner.

I would open 2,000 acres of ANWR to oil development and limit operations to late fall and winter when the caribou are not calving and less susceptible to disturbance. Furthermore, to ensure more than lip service to "environmentally responsible" development I would deploy principles four and five (see appendix). This means for example, establishing some form of Trustee/Oversight Board that would include subsistence and wilderness users, and representatives from the oil industry, the environmental communities as well as from the nearby native communities of Kaktovik and Arctic Village. The State of Alaska as well as the Interior Department would also be represented and play a key role. The board would act in an oversight capacity when it came to ensuring that discreet environmental goals i.e. caribou protection, pollution controls, water quality, were being followed in the design and operations of oil extraction. In regard to the trustee role, a certain percent of oil royalties would be dedicated to renewable energy and post-oil restoration activities. In setting up the "renewable resource" royalty, one could consider mimicking the arrangement Audubon had with Consolidated Oil and Gas (see p. 48) in that the stricter the operational stipulations, the lower the royalty. This arrangement would make it easier to accept the involvement and control of other public interests.

For those environmental readers still skeptical about my economic approach to opening ANWR, I call attention to the Nature Conservancy's operation of a 2,263 acre oil field in a swath of grasslands that is home to one of North's America's most endangered birds—the Attwater's prairie chicken. There are fewer than 40 birds left; yet instead of turning off the petroleum spigots, the Nature Conservancy drilled new gas wells. Niki McDaniel, spokesperson for the Texas Nature Conservancy, explains it this way, "We believe the opportunity we have in Texas City to raise significant sums of money for conservation is one we cannot pass up, provided we are convinced we can do this drilling without harming the prairie chickens and their habitat. And we are convinced."[186] While the environmental issues are dramatically different between Texas City and the Arctic Plain, the message here is that two environmental organizations—Nature Conservancy and Audubon—have shown that if done *right*, oil can mix with environmental protection.

As an Alaskan aware of directional drilling technology and the natural fluctuations and resiliency of caribou, the question for me is not can it be done *right*, but rather one of trust to do it right and is it worth it? I do not trust the Interior Department under the Bush administration to do it right alone—hence the importance of a functional Trustee/Oversight Board. And for me, it is certainly worth it from the long view home if ANWR serves as the political chit for moving us, as a nation, in the right direction on renewable energy and global warming. Taking the long view home, I am first a resident of planet Earth before I am Alaskan with environmental roots. Taking the long view home, I must be honest about how I live. Like many conservationists, I heat my home with oil and I drive a car getting 30 mpg at best. I am still a part of our petroleum-based economy.

Fortunately, we are changing. Many of us who engaged in issues popular in the 1960s and 1970s, such as peace, ecology and human rights are now choosing to live in a healthier and sustainable manner. According to market researcher and sociologist, Paul Ray, this group of American consumers has grown from 4 percent of the population in the 1960s to more than 24 percent in the 1990s, a new record for such a population trend.[187] He calls this demographically significant group of Americans the Cultural Creatives. "The appearance of the Cultural Creatives in America is a very hopeful thing for our society, for it offers a chance to create a more positive new culture," Ray notes in a 1997 issue of *American Demographics*.[188]

While this significant segment of our population is not organized or politically situated to make a difference on issues like ANWR, it is making a very significant difference in the marketplace. Monica Emerich, the Director of Research for a Natural Business magazine estimates that the total market for sustainable economy goods and services is *$76.5 BILLION dollars*. Here is how she breaks out the sustainable economy marketplace:

> Environmental Management and Audits $1.5 billion
> Energy Conservation Products/Services $1.0 billion
> Sustainable Manufacturing Processes $73.5 billion
> Websites, disks, videos etc. $920 million
> Books, audiocassettes and manuals $250 million[189]

The largest segment—sustainable manufacturing—includes recycled and recovered products in paper, textiles, plastics, glass, rubber and metals. Ms. Emerich also estimates that the market for natural and eco-products adds another $15.2 billion to the LOHAS Marketplace. LOHAS is the acronym for Lifestyles of Health and Sustainability.

It is this growing market that allows many of us to perform our daily activities of shopping, driving and turning on switches and all the while make a modest difference in promoting a sustainable economy. Instead of "think global, act local" we can now "think local and act global." You can go to the grocery store and buy food that has been independently certified to come from a sustainable food production system. In many regions, you can install small hydro operations or solar panels and become part of the "off the grid" lifestyle. You can take an eco-tour that supports low-impact indigenous communities. We can now do so much more than recycle bottles.

In my college days in the 1970s, I worked with a Ralph Nader group on gaining passage of Iowa's Bottle Bill. Now I work on increasing the market for sustainable wild salmon through the "sustainable" labeling program of the Marine Stewardship Council. Whether it be bottles or fish, whether it be recycling or sustainability, we have plenty of causes and plenty of ways to act through our wallets.

According to Ray, "when price and quality are equal, 76 percent of consumers would switch brands or retailers if a company were associated with a good cause."[190] Corroborating this finding is a recent study of the Hartman Group, a natural business market research firm based in Washington State. With price equal, they noted that 52 percent of Americans are very interested in buying green products.[191]

Equal to the impact of the marketplace in allowing us to "think local and act global" is the power of the Internet. Not only does the Internet bring the global marketplace into our homes, it brings the opportunity to network on a level that we never imagined. Through the Internet, I discovered the International Society of Ecological Economics and learned about their world conference in Canberra Australia. On a whim, I submitted an abstract for presenting a paper on eco-nomics. It was accepted, and soon I was on my way to the other side of the world to share my Alaskan-borne insights. I was taking my local experience global, and it was well received. Every time I share this story, I hear an equally amazing story in return. The world is literally at our fingertips.

It is this global perspective that makes it all the more important to take the long view home when engaged in local issues. Though I live hundreds of miles from the Arctic, the issue of ANWR visits me almost daily in my local newspaper. It feels like a local issue. And every time I return to my glacier, I see evidence of global warming. The retreat of the glacier is quite noticeable, and I know from reading the reports of the Juneau Icefield Research Project, an American Geographic Society project started in 1940s to study glacial formation, that the rate of retreat has accelerated in the last decade. The cores drilled in glacier ice tell the story of our dependence on wells drilled in oil. In thinking about the politicized issue of ANWR, I cannot ignore the global connection. It is a connection we need to keep making and making more often.

CHAPTER 11

Holding On to Leopold

The philosophical seeds of eco-nomic thinking are in these oft-quoted words of Leopold:

> "Examine each question in terms of what is ethically and esthetically right, as well as what is economically expedient. A thing is right when it tends to preserve the integrity, stability, and beauty of the biotic community. It is wrong when it tends otherwise."[192]

In conservation matters, a profit motive was not enough to justify decent land use for Leopold. Nor for that matter was a sentimental motive, as he warned his readers: "Conservation is paved with good intentions which prove to be futile, or even dangerous, because they are devoid of critical understanding of the land or of economic land use."[193] The land ethic Leopold espoused combined the practical and the emotional connection to the land with the intellect. His land ethic fused wise use and beauty into human occupation of the land. His land ethic is underlain by a fundamental respect for the integrity of nature.

Leopold's eloquent writing said it all in 1949. And as such, eco-nomics is not a new ethic, it's just another, more current twist on his Land Ethic. The challenge is bringing the Land Ethic into today's political and global world. That's the thinking behind eco-nomics—aiming to hold on to Leopold while applying him to the greater goal of global sustainability. Eco-nomics is a modest contribution toward this same objective. The twist on Leopold's Ethic is the global merging of capitalism and conservation. In the interest of holding on to Leopold, I offer these path markers on the road to sustainability and linkage.

> Principles of Eco-nomics
> 1—Conservation Is a Universal Value
> 2—Invest in "Ecologically Tuned In" Vested Interests
> 3—Provide a Forum to Advocate Balance
> 4—Compatibility Works
> 5—Maximize the Buy-In to Minimize the Conflict
> 6—Seek Local Solutions Based on Respect
> 7—Change Is a Given
> 8—Synergy Rules
> 9—Take the Long View Home
> (See appendix for complete listing of principles)

Successfully acting on these principles requires a spiritual foundation to nature in some form or another. The more we deepen our understanding of the job of living right with the land, the deeper our understanding of sustainability. We must see the job of living as part of our spiritual motivation for conservation actions. The job of living anchors the tree of sustainability. Or as better said by John Muir: "When a man plants a tree, he plants himself. Every root is an anchor, over which he rests with grateful interest, and becomes sufficiently calm to feel the job of living."[194]

Buddhist philosopher Tchih Nhat Hanh offers the Eastern translation of Muir's words:

> "If you are a poet you will see clearly there is cloud floating in this sheet of paper. Without a cloud there will be no rain; without rain the trees cannot grow; and without trees we cannot make paper. If we look even more deeply, we can see the sunshine, the logger who cut the tree, the wheat

that became his bread, and the logger's father and mother. Without all of these things, the sheet of paper cannot exist."[195]

Without the paper, the poet doesn't exist. Without the job of living, the tree of sustainability has nothing to sink its roots into. Without roots, the tree doesn't exist. Eco-nomics is a practical application of this poetic vision—helping to find roots of compatibility.

Eco-nomics is part of an emerging vision to see the whole forest and trees, including man in the trees. The application of these principles is open to all, including the logger who asks: "What good is an eagle if you can't eat it?" Yes, the logger behind the question may show a lack of respect or an inability to appreciate the integrity of the eagle and miss the point of Leopold's Land Ethic altogether. Nonetheless, he is part of the equation.

I am heartened to read that Carl Pope, Executive Director of the Sierra Club, recognizes the value of this human connection. In writing about the legacy of the protest demonstrations in Seattle, November of 1992, he states:

> "The autoworker who hunts or fishes on the weekend may well know the value of the woods as well as any Sierra Clubber. And the Sierra Clubber who goes to work on Monday morning has first-hand knowledge of how we all are "working harder for less." It's not that hard to look past the stereotypes to see a fellow citizen."[196]

The logger is part of my life in Southeast Alaska. A bigger part of my life is the Mendenhall Glacier. Whether I'm coming out of the grocery store or turning onto my street, the Mendenhall Glacier looms up ahead in chilling blue grandeur reminding me of the joy of living right with Alaska. In this cascading glacier, I also see vividly that change is a given; that change in tune with natural processes can be good. While the Mendenhall Glacier delivers this message to me in the course of everyday life, the visitor center delivers this ecological change message to the throngs of tourists descending from the gangplanks of floating cities. When the tourists visit the glacier they get reminded of their conservation values. I take away much more.

I go to my glacier for respite, for peace, for an opportunity to soak up some splendor and serenity. I go when I need to be reminded of my spiritual foundation in nature. I go to feel my spirit soar and sense the presence of greater forces at work. This is my church of the latter day glacier. This is where I pray that I too can make a difference like a leaf that floats down to rest on the massive tons of ice only to melt the ice underneath away through the mere heat of its tiny presence. I want my tiny presence to melt away the ice of polarized politics. This is where I pray for patience of voice . . . amidst the slow and eroding history of geology. This is where I pray for keen vision like that of the eagles soaring above the craggy pinnacles. This is where I pray for strength . . . amidst the adversity of the cold, biting winds. And on grand sunny days, this is where I pray that man and nature can harmoniously co-exist.

One day after returning from my church of the latter day glacier, I felt inspired to call Michael Silverstein (from chapter one and nine). I asked him why when linkage seems so obvious to us the voices of polarity are so strong? He acknowledged the same frustration and wondered if the war couldn't end by a simple declaration of what seemed apparent in the evolution of social, political, and economic thinking. Intrigued, I discussed what such a declaration would say. A few months later I received in the mail a draft declaration from Michael. I liked it immensely and couldn't help but try to embellish it; to weave in the principles of economics.

As authored by Michael Silverstein and edited by me, we offer this declaration for your dissemination. As you'll note, it is written so that everybody has a part to play on ending the war between the environment and business. Find where you fit. Say and act on your part then pass it on.

People's Declaration on Business and the Environment

1. *THE WAR* between American environmentalists and American business is over. Both sides hereby declare victory. Both sides declare conservation as a universal value. Both sides decide on a better way around the mutual impasse on progress. Here are the new roles for America:
2. *ENVIRONMENTALISTS* now recognize that the marketplace can be an equally, and at times more efficient, instrument of protective and restorative change than government regulation. Environmentalists accept that stewardship of natural resources is not exclusive to government; that ownership and vested interest can also lead to better stewardship. Environmentalists further recognize that change is a given and that we can begin to trust our growing knowledge of ecological systems and in this regard government and the science community have new responsibilities.
3. *RESOURCE INDUSTRIES* have learned that long-term economic viability rests with healthy, productive ecosystems; that their ecological roots must be recognized and protected. Resource dependent industries realize that adapting to the resource needs of other resource industries leads to a more stable economy and environment. Furthermore, these industries will take a practical, non-confrontational approach to proposals for new development or expansion; that they will seek to invite dialogue instead of inciting the ire of local environmentalists.
4. *ECONOMISTS* now acknowledge that environmental spending is not just a costly "end-of-pipe" way to cleaning air and water, but also a wonderful spur to innovation in materials, engineering and management that works to increase competitiveness and enhance national standards of living. Economists accept that

ecology is economy and that schools of thought such as Ecological Economics and Industrial Ecology must become part of the national discourse on economic policy.
5. *MANUFACTURERS* now understand that polluting less and recycling simply means becoming more efficient, less wasteful of energy and raw materials, and hence more profitable. CEOs now understand that through the global marketplace there is a natural synergy between capitalism and doing right by the environment.
6. *GOVERNMENT OFFICIALS* see a new primary role to play in the greening of the U.S. economy. It is a role away from command and control regulation and into promotion of the linkages between the economy and the environment. Officials pledge to seek new ways of solving resource problems through local solutions based on respect, through technological partnership with business and through changing the debate forum away from advocacy arenas.
7. *THE MEDIA* pledges to look a little deeper into the issues and be less swayed by the headline-grabbing battles of either/or ideologues engaged in the current controversy. The media also recognizes that most American people want and believe in both jobs and a healthy environment; that to always present the issue as environment versus economy is a disservice to the public and those trying to move forward together.
8. *THE INVESTMENT COMMUNITY* acknowledges that investing in companies that have not taken prudent steps to eliminate future environmental problems is just as much a prescription for disaster as not investing in companies that have not adequately addressed their retirement obligation. Investors now realize that good environment equals good business.
9. *THE AMERICAN PEOPLE* now know that to be given a choice of environment or economy is to be given a false choice. It is time to rise above the rhetoric of intolerance and instead activate

the language and forces of linkage. Give us real choices not just conflict. Let the economic environmental revolution roll on![197]

If this simple declaration seems trite or unnecessary, all one needs to do is examine recent national issues to see how the traditional thinking of business as evil and untrustworthy still derails progress. For example, in the mid-1990s, the Clinton administration was fairly close to striking a deal with the power industry over comprehensive emissions-trading program. According to a report in *Time* magazine (August 2002), major utilities were ready to agree to mandatory caps on emissions that included carbon (the pollutant most responsible for global warming). But first they wanted some certainty for their long-range planning and wanted the flexibility of buying and selling emissions rights. Believing that the market was just a sneaky way to avoid meeting the lower pollution caps, the environmental community strongly objected. In Katie McGinty's (then chair of Clinton's Council on Environmental Quality) own words, "Practically every utility in the country began to accept the notion that they would face legally binding carbon restrictions. But environmentalists who were opposed to doing anything consensual with industry said what we really should be doing is suing their butts under the current provisions of the Clean Air Act." The result today is that the EPA has no ability to regulate carbon and the plants are still spewing a raft of pollution.

This all-or-nothing approach must stop. It must be replaced by a platform of trust, reasonableness and cooperation. The People's Declaration on Business and the Environment is a place to start. It is one way to get us back to the wisdom of Leopold. It is a beginning for getting us further along in leaving future generations a more sustainable home.

If the sun is to shine upon our dreams of sustainability, we must dance in the simple joys of life with our neighbor, be they a corporate CEO or a tree hugger. And if we want this dance to be a dance of hope for our greater home called Earth, we need to reach out to the 72 percent of us who see conservation as a fundamental American value. Though the air and water is cleaner in many developed countries and we have more parks and preserves in protected status, our planet's most serious problems—global warming, loss of biodiversity, ocean pollution—remain daunting.

To face these serious challenges we must have more merging with our systems of action and change, not less. Economy with Ecology. Markets with Causes. Technology with Knowledge. Conservation with Community. Politics with Vision. Then and only then can we dance in hope of achieving sustainability. U.N. Secretary-General Kofi Annan believes in this dance when he notes in a *TIME* magazine special on planet Earth, "We have the human and material resources needed to achieve sustainable development, not as an abstract concept but as a concrete reality."[198]

May our children's children experience this reality? We will only get there if the environmental community accepts the leadership and partnership role of business and if the business community stops equating environmental concerns with job loss. We will only get there by accepting the People's Declaration on Business and the Environment. We will only get there by holding on to Leopold.

EPILOGUE

The Mountain Made Me Do It

I must tell my story of the mountain Denali . . . the mountain that honed my vision and gave me the courage and drive to complete this book. Twenty years ago I climbed Denali. I did not make the summit but I got the full Denali experience of the Earth's largest (note I am not saying tallest) mountain. Here is a shorter version of the essay I wrote upon my return from the mountain in 1982.

Mountains and milestones somehow seem to go together. Or is it mountains and molehills? I guess it just depends on where you are in your life. Well, I was crossing a milestone—entering the over-30-can't-be-trusted generation, and decided to add a mountain to it. So I turned to a majestic mountain that had always captured my awe; I turned to Denali (Mount McKinley for those of lower 48 background). At 20,320 feet, Denali is North America's highest mountain, commanding a position of majestic dominance in the rugged Alaska range.

Knowing that it was an expedition climb requiring 20 or so days, I set out diligently to get in shape . . . I wasn't going to let my older-generation body keep me from the summit. So, I worked out in the pool, I worked out at home, but most of all I worked out on the stairs. Stair streets are abundant in Ketchikan. So every day I ran up and down 77 stairs, 10 consecutive times; first carrying nothing on my back than carrying up to 60 pounds. Needless to say, I had many old timers scratching their heads in bewilderment . . . no one goes up and down the stairs in Ketchikan just for the hell of it.

Complete with my unique Ketchikan conditioning, I joined nine men for a guided climb up the West Buttress route of Denali. Mentally, physically, and emotionally I was charged with excitement when the ski plane landed at 7,000 feet. I was ready to go, ready to meet my Denali challenge. But I had to wait, as only half of our party made it into base camp before the weather window closed.

The international scene at base camp was entertaining. The French, German, Japanese, Canadian and American climbers were passing time by telling stories. Inevitably, the stories evolved into a game of match this feat. Listening to their tales I felt that what I was doing was of little consequence . . . except to me and those with whom I share my life . . . which after all is where consequences are best defined. Consequences like beauty are relative. Do you know of a better way to turn thirty—go up the hill and not over the hill? With this sense of personal consequence, inner peace, and excitement, my climb was soon underway.

As we ten Americans headed up the entryway glacier, Kahiltna Glacier, so too did the German Alpine Club. It was evident by their pace that we were going to have German neighbors throughout our ascent. At first I was a bit dismayed not to have my ultimate Alaskan mountain more to myself like my other Alaskan adventures. Eventually, I warmed up to the idea of combining wilderness adventure with international interaction.

We spent the next nine days setting up four camps until we reached the 14,000-foot level. On an expedition climb, the amount of gear, food and reserves requires two trips between each camp, with each climber carrying a pack and pulling a sled. The days alternated between blistering hot, clear, windless, days to intermittent cloud cover and wind. Like Everest, Denali's geographical position, size and prominence can generate its own weather patterns. Between the mountain massif and the heat reflection from the snow and ice, climbing on Denali can feel similar to climbing a volcano in the tropics even though the temperature is only twenty degrees Fahrenheit. But at night there is absolutely no resemblance to tropical volcanoes. Then you know you are very much on an Alaskan mountain with -20°F a common temperature.

Life at 14,000 feet brings on a mixture of summit fever, high-altitude weariness and spiritual giddiness. Everyone hangs out for a while to make an attitude and an altitude adjustment. Ah, attitude adjustments—you can never escape them—from the office to home and now to the mountain. Self-confidence gained from the lower half of the mountain must be checked with humility and courage for the formidable half of the remaining mountain. The attitude adjustment requires going within you, but the altitude adjustment is solely in the realm of the mountain—adjusting to the thin air created by the mountain's height. Regardless of your conditioning, altitude sickness can be the extent of your adjustment. Hanging out at 14,000 feet is like waiting for the mountain spirits to select who'll have the privilege of final ascents. Luckily for us, our entire climbing party passed the altitude adjustment. With attitude and altitude adjustments complete, I felt the charge of summit fever kindling in my bones.

During our climb to 17,300 feet, our guide remarked that this would not be a summit day for anybody. The wisps of cirrus, ponytail clouds signaled a dramatic change of weather. Sure enough the wind picked up momentum. We dug our tents in deep and built wind walls out of the hard encrusted snow. Fortified with snow anchors, ice axes, and wind walls, we set in to wait for the real storm due to come. With the surprise of a five-star alarm, the wind blasted in at 100 plus mph. "Emergency!" screamed the wind.

"Gear down for the worst," barked our leader Nick. We all scurried about inside our tents, putting all our clothes on and tying the sleeping bags up for quick evacuation. In the first hour, the wind shredded our tent fly. Grinding the snow to the consistency of powder and blowing it in through the seams, the wind actually made it snow inside the tents. Nick went out to check the tents and returned with the news that the German tents were blown away and that they still had not returned from their grossly miscalculated attempt on the summit. During the early hours of the storm, we all worried about the Germans, but as the mania of the wind jostled us relentlessly, our worries switched to ourselves . . . from concern of fellow man to self-concern . . . "Forget the Germans! How in the hell would we get out alive?" The storm continued for many, many more hours of madness.

With my body braced against the side of the tent, my head was being battered around like a basketball in a loose ball scramble. Bouncing head, howling winds, guide complaining about foolish Germans, I had nowhere to go to escape this maddening scene but deep inside myself. I sought my core strength, trying to hold back the sense of doom and panic that slithered in on the edges of my sanity. My survival mantra to myself went along these lines:

"I am going to make it through this storm. I have too much of life left to live. I have the seeds for great accomplishments in my field. I will have children. I will be a bridge of harmony for man and nature. I will be a voice of linkage for the environment and the economy. I want and will have children. I must and I will live through this hell of Denali's furor. I have too much purpose of life yet to live."

As soon as I would find some mental safe place to hold on to, a vicious round of high-velocity blasts would turn my head back into that basketball loose on the court. Thirty minutes later I'd catch my head again and hold on to it for another search of inward calm and courage. Whenever the wind speed dipped down to 50- to 60-mph gusts, someone would sigh "ahh." And as if the wind heard the "ahh," the wind would roar back to 80 to 100 mph and slap us with another mad scramble, tumble . . . only now I was inside that loose basketball. Would it ever end? I looked to Nick. But he just kept complaining that he was tired of carrying dead Germans off this mountain. No help there. Back inside myself was the only place to go. Oh well, I would just repeat my survival conversation endlessly to myself: I have too much purpose of life yet to live.

At 5 a.m., the Germans returned in a world of hurt. Now the concern for fellow man came rushing in on all of us. We evacuated our tents to help. The minute we stepped outside, the winds snatched our tents away with a roar. Tents gone, we turned to the snow cave inhabited by five other climbers. Through a lot of tenacity and adrenaline we somehow, albeit a bit miraculously, turned a five-person snow cave into an eighteen-person snow cave. I dubbed this emergency drill, "ice condo cram." We spent the next day and night safe from the howling, relentless wind, but I found the entrapment in a claustrophobic cave with eighteen others, some of whom were in harm's way (the Germans), equally maddening to the previous night. For another night, I drew upon my inner reserves of love, family, friends, and dreams. Dreams worked the best this night. Dreams of being back in loved one's arms, dreams of having children, dreams of career accomplishments that were due to come my way . . . dreams of being down off Denali. I fell asleep repeating my survival mantra. "I will have kids. I will be a voice of harmony. I have too much purpose of life yet to live."

The next day the winds were only gusting at sixty miles per hour. We considered this a lull in which to get the wounded Germans down to helicopter landings at 14,000 feet. There was no longer any talk of the summit. Not even a whisper. It was clear to all without a word to be said that it was time to get the hell out of high-altitude, high-velocity hell. Scamper we did. What took us 19 days to go up, took us two days to go down.

Upon my return, my husband asked the question I was ready for, "What did you decide about kids. Do you want to start a family now?" "Children? Children?" I teasingly pondered, then exploded with "Yes, I want children now!" There was no longer any hesitation about my immediate wants or goals in life. I went after them all with renewed vigor. I said "Yes!" to everything.

To our pleasant surprise, I soon became pregnant. Tracing back the day of conception, we learned that we conceived our first born the day after my return from Denali. Denali was consequential to me in ways I never imagined or expected, and it didn't take long before the consequences began to show. Soon came the stares and comments of surprise, "You're pregnant? Didn't you just come back from your climb?" To which I would serenely respond, "The mountain made me do it—never underestimate the power of mountains and milestones in your life."

Years later with two healthy children, I thought I was done with mountains and milestones, but I wasn't. I had always held on to the dream of building a bridge of harmony between man and nature. But since the climb, I have had more than my share of career-path setbacks. In an effort to let go of some disappointments, I then began to write this book. But that too began to seem a goal beyond my reach as the publishing rejections started coming in. I was ready to give up . . . wanted to give up. But then the mountain came back into my life.

During one of my deeper down cycles, we went on a family reunion camping trip. Being mostly an Alaskan family, we invariably ended up camping at Denali National Park. As the mountain poked through the clouds at the Eielson Visitor Center, I found myself telling the children around me (nieces and nephews too) my Denali story. I was able to point out how high I had gone. I was able to tell them of the inner belief that kept me strong so high up there in the jet stream storm.

For the first time in many years, I felt the pull of the second half of my survival chant: "I will be a bridge of harmony for man and nature. I will be a voice of linkage for the environment and the economy." I couldn't help but wonder why, if the first part came true so soon after my climb, the second part hadn't come true? Why hadn't I found the top-notch, pivotal policy job, why hadn't I found a publisher? Could the mountain be wrong? It seemed unlikely as I looked into the eyes of the children around me. As I told my survival story to the next generation, I resolved then and there that I would try again to find a publisher; that I would write my book . . . if for nothing more than to be at peace and fulfillment with the mountain, Denali, with the mountain glowing mightily on the horizon, with the mountain of my life's milestones.

But of course I am writing for more than just inner peace and fulfillment. I'm writing to articulate nine principles of eco-nomics through the stories of Alaska, through the experience of the West, and through the wisdom and research of professionals. I am writing to convey a vision of eco-nomics for the next century. Nonetheless, in the course of rejection, writing, revision, and resubmission, Denali has been my source of perseverance. I hold this book in my hand and once again say: "The mountain made me do it."

ENDNOTES

1. Jay Hammond, *Tales of a Bush Rat Governor* (Seattle: Epicenter, 1994), 167.
2. Truett Anderson, "There's No Going Back to Nature," *Mother Jones*, September 1996, 34.
3. Ibid.
4. Wirthlin Worldwide, "Environmental Update," *The Wirthlin Report*, Nov. 2000, Vol. 10, No. 8 wirthlin.com/publicns/reports.htm.
5. Ibid.
6. Michael Silverstein, *The Environmental Economic Revolution* (New York: St. Martin's, 1993), 26.
7. "Know Thine Enemy," *Earth Matters*, with Sharon Collins, Cable News Network, Inc, 1993, Transcript 12.
8. "Defending the Environmental Agenda," Editorial, *Sierra*, March 1995, 16.
9. Al Gore, New foreword to *Earth in the Balance*, April 23, 2000.
10. Presidential Debate at Wake Forest University, Oct. 11, 2000, excerpt available at www.issues2000.org/George_W_Bush_Environment.
11. Ibid.
12. Ibid.
13. *Washington Post*, p. A6, April 4, 2000.
14. Curtis Wilkie, *Boston Globe,* p. A16, Oct. 31, 2000.
15. *Washington Post*, p. A6, April 4, 2000.
16. Chris Smith, "Greening the Economy," *New Statesman & Society*, p. 16, February 1996, 26.
17. "Know Thine Enemy," *Earth Matters*.
18. Richard Stapleton, "Greed versus Green," *National Parks*, November 1992, 32.
19. Jill Hamburg, "The Lone Ranger," *California Magazine*, November 1990, 92-93.

[20] Joan Hamilton, "To Save America's Wilds," *Sierra*, September 1992, 11.
[21] Mark Mardon, "Madam President," *Sierra*, January 1994, 17.
[22] Chuck Cushman, "You've Heard the Problem: Here's the Solution," *Resource Development Council for Alaska*, Anchorage, 20 November 1992.
[23] George W. Bush, "Renewing America's Purpose" speech given at Sand Harbor June 1, 2000, excerpt at www.issues2000.org/George_W_Bush_Envronment.
[24] Al Gore, New foreword to *Earth in the Balance*, April 23, 2000.
[25] Pat Murphy, "Environment Moves Into Presidential Spotlight," *Environmental News Network*, August 10, 2000.
[26] Ibid.
[27] David B. Rockland, and Gwyn L. Fletcher, "The Economy, the Environment and Public Opinion: Most Americans Feel We Can Have Both Jobs and the Environment," *EPA Journal*, Fall 1994, 39.
[28] "America and the Environment: The Sky Isn't Falling," *Home Mechanix*, September 1994, 12-13.
[29] League of Conservation Voters, "Clean Air and Water are among Top Concerns for American Voters," *VoteEnvironment.Org* March 9, 2000.
[30] Wirthlin Worldwide, "Environmentalism: No Letting Up," *The Wirthlin Report Online*, August 1997, wirthlin.com/publicns/reports.htm.
[31] Wirthlin Worldwide, "Environmental Support Softens Amid Economic Uncertainty," *The Wirthlin Report Online*, September 1998, wirthlin.com/publicns/reports.htm.
[32] CNN News Network, Exit Polls, November 8, 2000, available at www.cnn.com/ELECTION/2000/epolls.
[33] Margot Higging, "Election 2000: Gray Day or Heyday for Greens?" *Environmental News Network*, Nov. 9, 2000.
[34] Harris Poll, *Business Week*, July 21-23, 2000.
[35] Pat Murphy, "Environment Moves Into Presidential Spotlight." *Environmental News Network*, August 10, 2000.
[36] Eugene Linden, "The Green Factor," *Time*, 12 October 1992, 58.
[37] Wirthlin Worldwide, "Environmental Update," *The Wirthlin Report*, Nov. 2000, Vol. 10, No. 8, wirthlin.com/publicns/reports.htm.
[38] George Pettinico, "The Public Opinion Paradox: Most of Us are Environmentalists—Until We Get to the Voting Booth," *Sierra*, November 1995, 28.

[39] Wirthlin Worldwide, "The Environment: Risky Business," *The Wirthlin Report*, Nov. 1999, Vol. 9, No. 9.
[40] Wirthlin Worldwide, "Environmental Support Softens."
[41] Wirthlin Worldwide, "Environmental Trends," *The Wirthlin Report Online*, October 1996, wirthlin.com/publicns/reports.htm.
[42] CNN News Network, Exit Polls, Nov. 8, 2000, available at www.cnn.com/Election/2000/epolls.
[43] Harris Poll, "Harris Feel Good Index," May 4-8, 2000.
[44] Jill Hamburg, "The Lone Ranger," 93.
[45] Kate O'Callaghan, "Whose Agenda For America?" *Audubon*, September 1992, 84.
[46] Jon Roush, "Up Front," *Wilderness*, Spring 1994, 3.
[47] Gallup Poll, April 3-9, 2000, available at www.polingreport.com/enviro.
[48] Editor, "Environmental Time Ear," *Los Angeles Times Editorial*, 1 May 2001.
[49] G.F. White, "Reflections on Changing Perceptions of the Earth," *Annual Review of Energy and the Environment*, 19, 1-13.
[50] Scott Sonner, "Recreational Fishing Becoming Lucrative Business All Over West," Associated Press, *Juneau Empire*, 1 March 1998, ???.
[51] Gary Polakovic, "Landmark Bill to Protect Ocean Fish is Signed," *Los Angeles Times*, 2 October 1998, A31.
[52] Mick Kronman, "Keeping It Clean," *National Fisherman*, October 1997, 28-33.
[53] Dennis Eames, Personal Communication, Southeast Alaska Seiners Association, 1987-1989.
[54] Ibid.
[55] Ibid.
[56] Alaska Department of Natural Resources, *Alaska Forest Practices Act Review: Final Report*, June 1989, 7-8.
[57] *Forest Wars*, Videocassette, Dir. Nicolas Brown, Produced for Earth Vision Institute by Summit Films, Inc., 1996, 72 min.
[58] Wallace Kaufman, *No Turning Back* (New York: Harper Collins, 1992), 137.
[59] Joseph L. Bast, Peter J. Hill and Richard C. Rue, *Eco-Sanity: A Common-Sense Guide to Environmentalism* (London: Madison Books, 1994), 193.
[60] _____, *Eco-Sanity*, 193.

[61] Terry L. Anderson and Donald R. Teal, *Free Market Environmentalism* (Boulder: Westview Press, 1991), 90.
[62] Riki Ott, Personal Interview, Anchorage, 5 September 1997.
[63] E.P. Odum, *Fundamentals of Ecology* (Philadelphia: W.B. Saunders Company, 1971), 148.
[64] Ibid., 228.
[65] Ibid., 229.
[66] Steve Colt, "The Economic Importance of Healthy Ecosystems," Institute of Social and Economic Research paper, *www.iser.uaa.alaska.edu*, 2 January 2001, 8.
[67] Linda Blum, interview, "Sierra Nevada Alliance," *Living On Earth*, Washington D.C., National Public Radio, 25 November 1994.
[68] "Sierra Nevada Alliance."
[69] Steve Tachera, interview, "Hamas Extinction," *All Things Considered*, Washington D.C., National Public Radio, 29 January 1997.
[70] Rich Richens, Personal Communication, 1997-1998.
[71] Kensington Mine Project Newsletter, Winter, 1997.
[72] Doug Mertz, Personal Communication, 1997-1998.
[73] Murray Walsh, Personal Communication, October 1998.
[74] Gail Bingham, *Resolving Environmental Disputes: A Decade of Experience* (Washington D.C., Conservation Foundation, 1986), 114.
[75] Lisa Jones, "Some Not-So-Easy Steps to Successful Collaboration," *High Country News*, 13 May 1996.
[76] _____, "Howdy, Neighbor! As a Last Resort, Westerners Start Talking to Each Other," *High Country News*, 13 May 1996.
[77] *Western Governors Association Enlibra Doctrine*, Washington D.C., 23 Feb. 99, www.westgov.org/Enlibra.
[78] Lisa Jones, "Howdy, Neighbor!"
[79] Elizabeth Arnold, "Watershed Council," *National Public Radio*, aired 28 June 2000.
[80] Ibid.
[81] Jon Maryolis, "How a Foe Saved the Quincy Library Group's Bacon," *High Country News*, 29 September 97, 13.
[82] Ed Marston, "The Timber Wars Evolve into a Divisive Attempt at Peace," *High Country News*, 29 September 97, 9.

83. *Forest Wars*, videocassette.
84. Ed Marston, "The Timber Wars Evolve," 8-9.
85. Chris Maser, *Resolving Environmental Conflict: Towards Sustainable Community Development* (Delray Beach, Florida: St. Lucie Press, 1996), 23.
86. William Krueger, "Managing Coalition Groups Effectively," *Journal of Forestry*, August 94, 8.
87. Ed Marston, "The Timber Wars Evolve," 10.
88. Ibid., 11.
89. Ibid.
90. Jim Lyons, interview with Ed Marston, "We May Be Seeing the Devolution of the Environmental Movement," *High Country News*, 29 September 1997, 9.
91. Maryolis, "How a Foe Saved the Quincy Library Group's Bacon."
92. Diane Feinstein, Letter, 4 December 1997, glg.org.
93. Michael Jackson, interview with Ed Marston, "We're much stronger together," *High Country News*, 29 September 1997, 13.
94. Wirthlin Worldwide, "Environmental Support Softens."
95. Patti Sherlock, "Idaho Learns to Share Two Rivers," *High Country News*, 13 May 1996, 9.
96. Elizabeth Arnold, "Watershed Council," *National Public Radio*, aired 28 June 2000.
97. Suzanne Iudicello, Personal Interview, 10 September 1995.
98. Power, Thomas, "The Wealth of Nature: Environmental Quality, Not Mining, Logging or Ranching, is Driving the Local Economic Development of the West," *Issues in Science and Technology*, Spring 1996, 48.
99. *Forest Wars*, videocassette.
100. Terry Terhar, "I Was Always Welcomed There," interview with Ed Marston, *High Country News*, 29 September, 12.
101. Greg Brown, "Executive Summary: Community Quality of Life Study," Alaska Pacific University, 25 June 1999.
102. Daniel Glick, "Having Owls and Jobs Too," *National Wildlife*, August 1995, 9-13.
103. Ibid.

104 Charles Harris, William McLaughlin and Greg Brown, "Rural Communities in the Interior Columbia Basin—How Resilient Are They?" Journal of Forestry, March 1998, 11-15.
105 Power, "The Wealth of Nature."
106 David M. Smith, *The Practice of Silviculture*, 7th ed (New York: John Wiley & Son, Inc., 1962), 327.
107 Wallace Kaufman, *No Turning Back* (New York: Harper Collins, 1994), 95.
108 Steven Yaffee et al, *Ecosystem Management in the United States, An Assessment of Current Experience* (Washington D.C.: Island Press, 1996), 17-39.
109 Ibid.
110 Hal Salwasser, "Ecosystem Management: Can It Sustain Diversity and Productivity?" *Journal of Forestry*, August 1994, 9.
111 Bill McKibben, "An Explosion of Green," *The Atlantic Monthly*, April 1995, 63.
112 Margot Roosevelt, "The Winds of Change," *Special Report Time*, 26 August 2002, A43.
113 Paul Hawken, "Toward a Restorative Economy," *Natural Life Magazine*, July 1995, www.life.ca.
114 Bob Hall, *Gold and Green* (Durham: Institute for Southern Studies), 1994, 4-6.
115 _____, "Study Disposes 'Jobs vs. Environment' Myth; States Ranked on Economic and Ecological Health," press release, Institute for Southern Studies, 1994.
116 Stephen Dill, "Environment, Jobs Go Together," Associated Press, *Juneau Empire*, 12 October 1994.
117 E.B. Goodstein, *Jobs and the Environment: The Myth of a National Trade-Off* (Washington D.C.: Economic Policy Institute), 4-33.
118 Bruce Lippke and Holly Fretwell, "The Market Incentive for Biodiversity," Journal of Forestry, January 1997, 4-7.
119 Robert Neuwirth, "Businesses Discover It Pays to be Green," *Natural Life Magazine*, January 1997.
120 Eric Roston, "New War on Waste," *Special Report Time*, 26 August 2002, A28.
121 Michael Silverstein, *The Environmental Revolution* (New York: St. Martin's, 1993), 29.

122 Ibid.
123 Joseph Romm, interview by Steve Curwood, *Living on Earth*, National Public Radio, 10 March 1995.
124 Harris Collingwood, "Is Environmental Protection Really Bad for Business?" *Working Woman*, June 1996, 14.
125 Rahul Jacob, "Corporate Reputations," *Fortune*, 6 March 1995, 54-61.
126 Ibid.
127 Barbara Kruwisiek, "The Emergence of a New Era in Mutual Fund Investing: Socially Responsible Investing Comes of Ages," Journal of Investing, Winter 1997, 8.
128 "The Business Charter for Sustainable Development: Principles for Environmental Management," International Chamber of Commerce, www.iccwho.org.
129 Ken Scott, *A Case Example: Hewlett Packard Company*, Calvert Social Research Investment Fund, 1 August 1996, cts.com.
130 Robert Neuwirth, "Businesses Discover It Pays to be Green."
131 Coalition for Environmentally Responsible Economies, *Annual Report 97*, cees@igc.org.
132 Jeffrey Kluger and Dorfman, Andrea, "The Challenges We Face", *Special Report Time*, 26 August 2002, A12.
133 Eric Lucas, "Resource Management," *Alaska Airlines Magazine*, November 1997, 27.
134 Pax World Fund, "Pax Watch Fund Rated Among Top Balanced Funds," paxfund.com/pwfpage.htm.
135 Eric Roston, "New War on Waste," *Special Report Time*, 26 August 2002, A31.
136 Forest Stewardship Council, "Making Its Mark," fsc@laneta.apc.org.
137 Jeff Bernard, "The Green Movement Meets the Timber Industry," Associated Press, *Juneau Empire*, 10 November 1997.
138 Neil Ulman, "Going Green—A Maine Forest Firm Prospers by Earning Eco-Friendly Label," *Wall Street Journal*, 26 November 1997.
139 Ibid.
140 Marc Levinson, "Seeing Red Over Green," *Newsweek*, 17 June 1996, 55.
141 *Eco Trust: 1996 Annual Report*, www.ecotrust.org.
142 Ibid.

[143] Elizabeth Manning, "A Chicago Bank Will Try to Invigorate Willapa Bay," *High Country News*, 17 March 1997.
[144] Anne Marie Janson et al., *Investing in Natural Capital, The Ecological Economics Approach to Sustainability* (Washington D.C., Island Press, 1994), 4.
[145] France Beguette, "A Budding Romance Between Industry and the Environment?" *The UNESCO Courier*, February 1993, 29.
[146] Todd Jefferson Moore, *In the Heart of Wood* (Seattle: Rain City Projects, ???).
[147] France Begutte, "A Budding Romance."
[148] "Dollars, Sense and Salmon," Editorial, *The Idaho Statesman*, 20 July 1997.
[149] Jack Hope, "Green Watch: Does Environmentalism Cost?" *Good Housekeeping*, February 1993, 116.
[150] *New Bearings: The Strategic Vision of EcoTrust* (Portland:EcoTrust, 1993).
[151] Truett Anderson, "There's No Going Back to Nature," *Mother Jones*, September 1996, 34.
[152] Georgia Stele, "Billy Frank, Jr., Tribal Salmon Advocate," *Pacific Fishing*, June 1997, 23.
[153] Wallace Kaufman, *No Turning Back* (New York: Harper Collins, 1994), 175.
[154] Bast et al., *Eco-Sanity*, 51.
[155] Wirthlin Worldwide, "Environmentalism: No Letting Up." 1997.
[156] Wirthlin Worldwide, "The Precautionary Principle: Throwing Science Out With the Bath Water," *Issues Perspective*, February 2000.
[157] Paul Ehrlich and Anne Ehrlich, *Betrayal of Science and Reason* (Washington D.C.: Island Press, 1996), 19.
[158] Wallace Kaufman, *No Turning Back*, 129.
[159] "Playing With Fire," Editorial, *Denver Post*, 23 October 1998, 6B.
[160] David Helvarg, *The War Against The Greens* (San Francisco: Sierra Club Books, 1997), 13.
[161] Jay Hammond, *Tales of a Bush Rat Governor*, 175.
[162] _____, Personal Interview, Anchorage, 26 August 1997.
[163] _____, 177.
[164] _____, 318.
[165] Gore, *Earth in the Balance*, 187-189.
[166] Denis Hayes, Personal Interview, Seattle, 17 November 1997.

[167] Daniel McGinn, "The New Ford," *Newsweek*, 23 November 1998, 56-58.
[168] Denis Hayes, Personal Interview, Seattle, 17 November 1997.
[169] Paul Roberts, "The Great Green Hope," *Seattle Weekly*, 20 January 1993, 19.
[170] Denis Hayes, 1997 President's Report: Climate Changes & Solar Energy: Lessons from the Computer Revolution," *Bullitt Foundation News*, info@bullitt.org.
[171] Carol M. Browner, "The Common Sense Initiative: A Generation of Environmental Protection," speech, Center for National Policy Newsmaker Luncheon, Washington D.C., 20 July 1994.
[172] Michael Silverstein, Personal Interview, 4 January 1998.
[173] Al Gore, "Finding a Third Way," *Newsweek*, 23 November 1998, 58.
[174] Eric Roston, "New War on Waste," *Special Report Time*, 26 August 2002, A28.
[175] Silverstein, *The Environmental Economic Revolution*, 19-25.
[176] Ibid.
[177] Daniel Zwerdling, "This Week," *NOW with Bill Moyers*, Public Broadcasting Service, 6 September 2002.
[178] Ben Speis, "Sanctuary or Solution," *Anchorage Daily News,* 15 April 2001, A8-10.
[179] Ibid.
[180] National Resources Defense Council, Press Release, "NRDC Says Energy Bill Promotes True Energy Security, 27 February 2002.
[181] Margot Roosevelt, "The Winds of Change," *Special Report Time*, 26 August 2002, A44.
[182] Jennifer Peter, "Bush Urged To Address Global Warming," Associated Press story in *Juneau Empire,* 17 July 2002, 7.
[183] Christine Todd Whitman, "A Strong Climate Plan," *Special Report Time*, 26 August 2002, A48
[184] H. Josef Hebert, "ANWR: How Many Jobs Will It Produce?" Associated Press, reported, *Juneau Empire,* 12 March 2002, 7.
[185] Alision Balie et al., from Tellus Institute and Goldberg, Marshall from MRG & Associates, *Clean Energy: Jobs for America's Future*, a study prepared for World Wildlife Fund, October 2001.

[186] Janet Wilson, "Nature Conservancy's Alliance Raise Hackles," *The Los Angeles Times,* 1 September 2002.
[187] Monica Emerich, "LOHAS Means Business," *Lohas Journal,* March 2000, 32-34.
[188] Paul Ray, "Who Is the LOHAS Consumer?" *LOHAS Journal,* March 2000, 35-52.
[189] Ibid.
[190] Emerich, "LOHAS Means Business."
[191] Ibid.
[192] Aldo Leopold, *A Sand County Almanac* (New York: Oxford University Press, 1949), 224-225.
[193] Curt Meine, *Aldo Leopold: His Life and Work* (Madison: University of Wisconsin Press, 1988), 503.
[194] Gene Wood, "Establishing a Conservation Philosophy," *Journal of Forestry,* January 1995, 6.
[195] Asta Bowen, "How an Eco-Logger Vic92 ws I Iis Work," *High Country News,* 24 November 1997, 16.
[196] Carl Pope, "Seattle's Legacy," Newsletter—Vol. 2, No. 1, Alliance for Sustainable Jobs and the Environment.
[197] Gene Wood, "Establishin1g a Conservation Philosophy," *Journal of Forestry,* January, 1995, 7.
[198] Kofi Annan, "Beyond the Horizon," *Special Report Time,* 26 August 2002.

APPENDIX A

Eco-nomic Principle No. 1
Conservation Is a Universal Value

Equality, Justice, and Freedom are core values of Americans. While we may disagree as to the application of these values in particular circumstances, we agree that these are shared values among our neighbors. It is time to recognize that after decades of inspirational writing from Thoreau to John Muir, after a half-century of national leadership from Theodore Roosevelt to Al Gore, and after the 1970s sweep of environmental laws, conservation is also a core value of most Americans. The desire for conservation is no longer confined to *Field and Stream* readers, to viewers of PBS "Nature" and to LL Bean shoppers. We all want the same thing—a job and the ability to raise a family in a clean and healthy environment. After all, two-thirds of most Americans consider themselves an environmentalist.

Eco-nomic Principle No. 2
Invest in "Ecologically Tuned In" Vested Interest

All renewable resource industries have a vested interest in the sustainability of the raw resource, such as timber, fish, and land. Some industries act responsibly in protecting this interest, others do not due to short-term perspectives or lack of vision. Acting responsibly means an industry recognizes their ecological roots and promoting appropriate environmental protection. These industries see that the environmental and economic agenda of resource politics can be one and the same, period. Privatization of access to public resources can lead to a stronger connection to the resource base and if designed correctly, a stronger tie to environmental protection. When the ecological and economic connection is made, vested interest can work to protect as well as to promote.

Eco-nomic Principle No. 3
Provide a Forum to Advocate Balance

The existing public process of "release a document and hold a public hearing" does not provide a forum for seeking balanced solutions or politically achievable compromises. Work sessions and informal conferences should be favored over the 5-minute "state your name for the record" drill. Public hearings are suitable for advocacy but not for conflict resolution. Any political advocate worth their salary will loyally spend their 5 minutes of public-hearing time advocating their organizational or business interest and not waste their allotted time on finding balance. Whenever possible, convene roundtable discussions. The convener of work sessions or roundtable discussions should be perceived as neutral and as a professional whose purpose is to be a neutral facilitator. This often excludes government agencies as neutral conveners. When this is recognized then the agency host actively participates and pays for the professional services. The time, setting and forum for public involvement must change if one wants open dialogue on ways to find balance. Give people a chance to check their advocacy at the door and talk as problem solvers. Once a conducive setting has been found, recognize that seeking common ground does not make one any less a conservationist or a development advocate.

Eco-nomic Principle No. 4
Compatibility Works

Like species sharing the same ecological niches, industries can share the same dependency on a healthy ecosystems. And similar to species, industries can find cooperative strategies that provide for mutual benefit. And as noted by Dr. E.P. Odum, who many view as the father of ecology, species diversity is directly correlated with ecosystem stability. Similarly, communities relying on multiple resource-dependent industries as opposed to a single extractive industry are economically more stable. Because the ecological base of one resource industry often overlaps into the base or area of another resource-dependent industry, seeking compatibility among resource industries can promote better management of that shared resource base. The web effect of shared economic and ecological systems makes seeking compatibility of resource-dependent industries a successful eco-nomic strategy. To ignore this web effect and not listen responsively to the needs of another resource-dependent industry can, as we know from the *Exxon Valdez,* have dire, costly consequences.

Eco-nomic Principle No. 5
Maximize the Buy-In to Minimize the Conflict

The more directly affected interests place their fingerprints on a proposed project or action, the less likely those interests will seek the lawsuit route. The more stakeholders buy in on either a procedural or substantive level, the more likely things can move forward out of court. If the right ingredients are present, seek formal collaboration of interests to resolve environmental or resource-use conflicts. Community-based collaboration is a growing alternative to lawsuits as more people learn that courts are not is the dispute-resolution business. Time not spending litigating and appealing is time being proactive together to discover common interests and solutions. Solutions agreed to by all stakeholders significantly enhance acceptance and implementation by legislative and/or administrative bodies. The more the buy in, the more likely the solution will stick.

Eco-nomic Principle No. 6
Seek Local Solutions Based on Respect

If we accept the idea that humans are part of ecosystems, then meaningful participation by those affected by the long-term health of that ecosystem is an essential element in any approach to ecosystem management. This drives ecosystem management and planning down to the local or regional level. Accepting this premise of human integration into ecosystem management should allow upper levels of management, both corporate and governmental, to accept a lower, locally generated solution. Getting to solutions invariably means resolving conflict. Progress in resolving conflict occurs when there is basic respect for the right and welfare of fellow human beings. The more problem-solving individuals see each other as neighbors needing to share the same ecosystem, the easier it is to let respect enter into the dispute and eventually become the glue that holds any agreement together. If all politics are local, why can't national political problems be solved locally? Go where the odds for respect prevailing are best; go where folks can appreciate that none of us are as smart as all of us; go local when given the chance.

Eco-nomic Principal No. 7
Change Is a Given

Understanding patterns of ecological change is part of promoting better environmental practices. Understanding the patterns of economic change is part of providing community stability. We can find solutions in mimicking or complementing the direction of change within the forests, the grasslands, and the oceans. Change is the dynamic constant in both ecological and economic systems. Therefore, fusing systems where possible and making changes beneficial to both man and nature is desirable and sometimes an achievable end. As the field of ecology branches out and grows into our everyday life, the real challenge here becomes one of trust to do right by man and nature; to practice ecosystem management and model sustainable development, knowing that we work and live in dynamic systems.

Eco-nomic Principle No. 8
Synergy Rules

In a fully evolved ecosystem, waste and pollution do not exist. What is waste to one species is food for another species. In a fully evolved economic system, what is one company's waste is another company's raw product material. Likewise, businesses that do not take advantage of green marketing, waste reduction, recycling, and energy efficiency will become the dead-end businesses of the new century. The new awakening in industry is about absorbing the lessons that should have been learned from nature long ago. Earth is in the hands of a more aware, enlightened species that as viewed Earth from a spacecraft. The "hands-off" approach to saving nature is not as effective as the "hands-on" approach. Proper use of the marketplace can accelerate the benefits back to the forests, mountains and oceans. Man and nature are forever entwined, as they exist now. There is *no going back* to nature. There is only going forward together. Prosperity for humankind can, if done wisely and compassionately, can be good for the environment.

Eco-nomic Principle No. 9
Take the Long View Home

Whenever possible, define the issue in as global a context as possible. Also, define the time horizon for accountability long enough to allow for the economic benefits of alternative design and mitigation to be counted for in the equation of jobs and the environment. Think as far down the line as the dynamics of the issue allows. The longer the horizon, the larger the window for finding and promoting synergy. And always keep within the notion of being a global citizen. Seize the opportunity to enlarge the debate both in time and scope. Cross over to the middle of the road and take the long view home when position and timing give you the chance to define the context of the debate.

ABOUT THE AUTHOR

Equipped with a Masters Degree from Yale School of Forestry and Environmental Studies Kate Troll set off in 1977 to begin her professional career in Alaska. Hired by Bristol Bay Native Association, Kate was the first person to introduce Coastal Zone Management to "Bush Alaska". After working for the local planning department in Ketchikan, she was elected to local office. In the 1980's and 90's she represented commercial fishing in the tumultuous world of 'fish politics' both in Alaska and at a national level. She was appointed to the first State Board of Forestry, has taught at the University of Alaska Southeast and held several resource policy positions with the State of Alaska. At the world conference of the International Society of Ecological Economics, Kate presented on paper on 'Eco-nomics'. Her outdoor pursuits parallel her intense professional journey. She has climbed Denali, paddled through the Gates of the Arctic, experienced whales diving under her kayak and skied through the Great Gorge of the Alaska Range.

BVG